Wikipedia and the Representation of Reality

This book presents a contemporary examination of what information is represented and discusses how that information is presented and who gets to participate (and serve as gatekeeper) in the world's largest online repository for information, Wikipedia.

Bridging contemporary education research that addresses the 'experiential epistemology' of learning to use Wikipedia with an understanding of how the inception and design of the platform assists this, the book explores the complex disconnect between the encyclopedia's formalized policy and the often unspoken norms that govern its knowledge-making processes. At times both laudatory and critical, this book illustrates Wikipedia's struggle to combat systemic biases and lack of representation of marginalized topics as it becomes the standard bearer for equitable and accessible representation of reality in an age of digital disinformation and fake news.

Being an important and timely contribution to the field of media and communication studies, this book will appeal to academics and researchers interested in digital disinformation, information literacy, and representation on the Internet, as well as students studying these topics.

Zachary J. McDowell is an Assistant Professor in the Department of Communication at the University of Illinois, Chicago. His research focuses on access and advocacy in digitally mediated peer production spaces. In particular, Zach's research focuses on digital literacy, self-efficacy, and how digitally mediated tools, particularly Wikipedia, shape these areas of inquiry.

Matthew A. Vetter is an Associate Professor of English and affiliate faculty in the Composition and Applied Linguistics PhD program at Indiana University of Pennsylvania. His research asks questions related to technology, rhetoric, and writing, with a specific interest in investigations of the ideological and epistemological functions of digital communities.

Wikipedia and the Representation of Reality

Zachary J. McDowell and
Matthew A. Vetter

First published 2022
by Routledge
605 Third Avenue, New York, NY 10158

and by Routledge
2 Park Square, Milton Park, Abingdon, Oxon, OX14 4RN

Routledge is an imprint of the Taylor & Francis Group, an informa business

Library of Congress Cataloging-in-Publication Data
Names: McDowell, Zachary J., author. | Vetter, Matthew A., author.
Title: Wikipedia and the representation of reality / Zachary J. McDowell and Matthew A. Vetter.
Description: New York, NY : Routledge, Taylor & Francis Group, 2022. | Includes bibliographical references and index.
Subjects: LCSH: Wikipedia. | Electronic encyclopedias—Social aspects. | Authorship—Collaboration—Social aspects. | Knowledge, Theory of—History—21st century.
Classification: LCC AE100 .M39 2022 (print) | LCC AE100 (ebook) | DDC 030—dc23
LC record available at https://lccn.loc.gov/2021031587
LC ebook record available at https://lccn.loc.gov/2021031588

ISBN: 978-0-367-55570-2 (hbk)
ISBN: 978-0-367-55571-9 (pbk)
ISBN: 978-1-003-09408-1 (ebk)

DOI: 10.4324/9781003094081

Typeset in Times New Roman
by codeMantra

Contents

Acknowledgments

First of all, we would have never gone down this path if not for being blessed with the good fortune to work with the wonderful people at the Wiki Education Foundation. Their hard work, dedication, and patience have been invaluable in our understanding of Wikipedia, its issues, and its complexity. We are all incredibly indebted to their kindness, support, and friendship. We are also grateful for the many students who have risen to the challenge of a Wikipedia-based writing assignment over the years, and who have taught us a great deal about how Wikipedia works, and how to teach writing and communication in the encyclopedia.

We are tremendously thankful for the support of our institutions to ensure the Creative Commons license of this publication. The Creative Commons license was partially funded by the University of Illinois at Chicago Library's Research Open Access Article Publishing (ROAAP) Fund, as well as funding from the College of Humanities and Social Sciences at Indiana University of Pennsylvania.

Of course, this book would not be possible without the dedication and resilience of the Wikipedia community.

A big thank you to David Solberg for his assistance with citation and reference work on this book manuscript as well as to our editorial assistant, Emma Sherriff at Taylor and Francis, for her patience and guidance throughout this process.

Preface

> If you want to master something, teach it.
>
> —Richard Feynman

> The scientist is not a person who gives the right answers, [they are the] one who asks the right questions.
>
> —Claude Levi-Strauss

This book came into being through years-long friendships and collaborations that emerged through our overlapping and mutual work with Wikipedia. We have utilized Wikipedia in education for nearly a decade – devoting countless hours employing Wikipedia in the classroom, in research, and in our social outreach. Our experiences as educators, as academics, and as Wikipedians have informed how we approach, understand, and critique Wikipedia. Connections through teaching turned into conference papers, which then turned into academic publications and volunteer outreach (often "Edit-a-Thons").[1] The topics we cover in this book, as well as those of our previous presentations and publications, emerged through conversations about our different ways of approaching shared experiences in which we reflected deeper together on these topics. While much of our experience that engendered our reflections in this book emerged from interactions with students (whether formally in a classroom or in a volunteer space), what we have realized is that the experiences of students on Wikipedia are that of new users, in general. In our experience of facilitating and attending Wikipedia editing events and workshops, we also see the experiences of students reflected in those of more diverse groups of academics and other professionals. Although we often will laud the educational benefits of working with Wikipedia in the classroom (whether for learning to write for a general audience, learning information literacy, or otherwise), not only are these experiences indicative of learnings for Wikipedia users, in general, but the purpose of this book is to reflect on not just the process of how Wikipedia represents reality but also the experience of participating in that process. So to this point, when we discuss students in relation to Wikipedia we envision a student as the novice or the lifelong learner, not necessarily the traditional classroom student.

In the following pages of this preface, we discuss our experiences of teaching users to edit and learn about Wikipedia, as these experiences shaped how we began to understand not only how Wikipedia *is supposed to work* but also how it *does work* in relation to the experience of learning to participate in the Wikipedia community. As Feynman famously said, "If you want to master something, teach it," and this is incredibly apt – not for the mastery of Wikipedia itself (who can say they have "mastered" Wikipedia?) but for the reflective moment to struggle with others in the understanding and explanation. These experiences helped to shape how we moved past simply understanding and explaining the stated goals, policies, and guidelines on Wikipedia. Instead, we read how Wikipedia "works" through understanding users' experiences of Wikipedia, both in how users grapple with stated guidelines and policy, but also the experience of dealing with the interface and the community. As Levi-Strauss suggests of us as academics and social scientists, we attempt to "ask the right questions." Writing on Wikipedia as a new user can be incredibly frustrating as the learning curve can be extremely high, and we have wrestled with numerous frustrations with those who we have guided. These frustrations come from all over, even with one of Wikipedia's earliest editing guidelines, the directive to "Be Bold" because students (and indeed any novice to Wikipedia) often face challenges when directed to "be bold" just to begin participating. Students also struggle to understand "Reliable sources" (WP:RELIABLE)[2] and "Verifiability" (WP:V)[3] – two key policies that shape how the community determines how raw data or information is filtered into knowledge. Furthermore, we know that newcomers to Wikipedia are also confused by "what counts" as knowledge – how do we determine what topics are notable enough in an encyclopedia with over 6 million articles? As if all of the above were not frustrating enough to keep all but the most diligent editors at bay, new editors also experience significant "gatekeeping" by seasoned editors, often invoking confusing and elaborate policy arguments which preclude novice participation. These discussions link to direct experiences we've each had, as we teach, train, and talk about Wikipedia with others in our immediate communities. They also link to the overall organization of this book, in which we provide a more nuanced exploration of how Wikipedia shapes its representation of reality.

While this book is not a collection of anecdotes about our experiences, our experiences as educators, academics, and volunteers provided the inspiration for our research. Between us we have trained thousands of students and other novices on how to engage with Wikipedia. Time and time again, we have experienced the struggles of new users, discussed these struggles, and helped to guide them through. Much of our understanding of the challenges faced by new users have emerged from these experiences, whether in a formal classroom or in a volunteer space as trainers. More often than not, our students were outside the typical demographic of Wikipedia editors and faced numerous obstacles and successes on their journeys to edit. Witnessing the incredible impact that Wikipedia has on our students, as well as that students have had on Wikipedia, we have each focused in different ways to engage Wikipedia as an open and collaborative knowledge production space. Students often have very little understanding of how Wikipedia works – most have never made an edit, let alone looked at a "talk" page[4] or non-mainspace page.[5] Students often assume that academics write Wikipedia, or that Wikipedia has professional writers. Despite an awareness that "anyone could edit Wikipedia," they simply just did not think about how it came together. Furthermore, despite using it constantly (many admit that they use it nearly daily) they recall being told "not to use it" not only for school papers, but, in general, since it was so unreliable. Our interactions with other teachers and academics at conferences and elsewhere have furthered this understanding. Many of the myths and misunderstandings of Wikipedia persist among academics, even those who study education, writing, digital culture, communication, and other relevant fields. As we reflected on this circumstance, it seemed that everyone was using Wikipedia despite being told not to, and no one knew how it worked.

While the average editor on Wikipedia is white and male, our students are majority women, many of them are non-white, and many are often non-native English speakers. Their experiences of Wikipedia are undoubtedly different from many of the editors, which both brings new perspectives to Wikipedia as well as often challenges many of the assumptions of veteran editors about the person editing.

Wikipedia's Expectation for Editor Confidence

One of the earliest editing guidelines in Wikipedia, "Be Bold" (WP:BOLD) has become something of a mantra among Wikipedia editors and is frequently invoked in training and other initiatives to familiarize the public with the encyclopedia. "Be Bold,"[6] asks potential editors to "Go for it." "Wikis like ours," the article further explains, "develop when everybody helps to fix problems, correct grammar, add facts, make sure wording is accurate, etc." For the encyclopedia to grow and improve, editors should be active in correcting issues or errors they notice. Additionally, the guideline warns, "Do not be upset if your bold edit gets reverted." Editors should "Assume Good Faith" (the good intentions of other editors) if and when their bold edits are removed.

At face value, "Be Bold" serves an important purpose in the Wikipedia community. The encyclopedia depends on volunteer editors to feel confident to constantly update, revise, and correct an already enormous (and growing) body of content.[7] At the same time, the underlying assumption in the bold directive, that such a disposition is equally available to all potential contributors, demonstrates a somewhat exclusive and even gendered ethos at work throughout Wikipedia.[8]

We bring a few different positionalities to the table. First, as academics we come with considerable intellectual interest in Wikipedia as a subject of study and fascination. We are Wikipedians, to an extent, in that we each have editorial experience and have contributed to the project's content.[9] But we are also educators and have spent years teaching Wikipedia-based assignments and helping students to become familiar with and contribute to the encyclopedia. It is this final role that has shown us, most explicitly, how the boldness directive fails to encourage or comfort new users. Because, of course, many new editors do not feel bold when first learning to edit, nor can they easily access that particular disposition.

We have had numerous interactions with students who have taken issue with the idea of being bold. One of our students likened the boldness directive to being "thrown in a pool without the ability to swim," while another noted that they "ultimately felt more anxiety than boldness." Students often felt like they were stepping on others toes, and were afraid to upset, anger, or disappoint the author of the original words. Feeling empathy for the original author's work, they realized that they too might feel upset by their words changed. In our experience, this sentiment most often emerged in female-identifying students, but also manifested in many students from other marginalized identities and positionalities.

As with reading Wikipedia, researching Wikipedia often means travelling down rabbit holes. As we continued to discuss and research, we discovered that Larry Sanger, one of the founders of Wikipedia, authored the original "Be Bold" page.[10] He begins by simply stating that "Wikis don't work if people aren't **bold**," which is indicative of the core expectation for editing Wikipedia. As one of the original "Editing Guidelines," it insists that one must "get out there and make those changes" and not "worry about their feelings," both statements which run counter to many students' (and many people's) sense of agency. To "Be Bold," users are encouraged to put aside feelings of reluctance, unfamiliarity, or discomfort about publicly contributing to the project, reflecting a view of agency to write, and be included that is not shared by all.

This became a sticking point for us, as we recognized that this is just the first stumbling block before any other issues that Wikipedia has. It helped us recognize that many of Wikipedia's inclusion issues lie in historical gendered systems that must be unfurled in their own right – Wikipedia is obviously a piece of this early internet utopianism and remains plagued by numerous masculinist ideals about participation. While many of the policies and guidelines of Wikipedia, particularly "Be Bold," remain well-intentioned, they were conceptualized without a greater understanding of how to be actively (rather than passively) inclusive of diverse participation and ideas.

As we discuss in Chapter 4, Wikipedia's "Be Bold" directive remains the first stumbling block, as you need to be bold enough to participate, and to continue to participate. In the end, we agree with the "spirit" of Be Bold. At a certain point, all editors have to take that final step and hit the "publish button" – but we have to also acknowledge that it remains double-edged like so many things on Wikipedia, as newcomers who are successfully emboldened can gain a sense of agency through their success, but newcomers who experience gatekeeping or hostility may experience a further lack of agency or feelings of failure from not being successful.

What Counts as Information

An historically mistrusted resource, especially in formal academic spaces, Wikipedia might be considered an odd platform to teach information literacy. Yet the encyclopedia has been both recognized and praised by many in recent years due to its ability, especially when compared to other digital communities, to ward off fake news and other types of problematic information.

As educators in communication, writing, and literacy, we have seen firsthand the difficulty that students have in understanding proper sources, and Wikipedia's construction of facts and truth through policies Reliability and Verifiability can be a struggle for many when faced with editing. On a basic level, students struggle with source evaluation and understanding when a source is credible, not to mention when a source is relevant and appropriate to use in the encyclopedia. However, it is through this struggle that students start to understand basic tenets of information literacy.

As is obvious, the information landscape has changed dramatically in the last two decades. The rapid rise of misinformation and disinformation in the contemporary media necessitates new approaches to understanding and processing information. Furthermore, rapid technological shifts in communication have made irrelevant our previous information literacy models. Students who were taught these models, further, are predisposed to evaluating sources, when they do evaluate them, in an isolated manner that focuses on the merits or weaknesses of a single text, without considering the larger context of that text both within and outside Wikipedia. Reliability in Wikipedia depends on independent, secondary, and high-quality sources, certainly, and those sources should be examined independently as part of a robust process of evaluation. However, it is ultimately communities, rather than individual authors or readers of sources that actually construct reliability. Wikipedia, while it may not be especially inviting at first, given the complexity and range of policy surrounding reliability, has developed such a community. Moreover, that community has a set of standards, processes, and policies that, taken together, demonstrate how the encyclopedia determines reliability. Asking students simply to begin to enter into this process and community is a worthwhile endeavor. Students transform their relationship to information through their interactions with Wikipedia, and in doing so, begin to understand reliability as a socially negotiated and distributed process.

Over the years, we've learned how to scaffold Wikipedia assignments so that students propose secondary sources and content additions before making edits to mainspace. This process allows us as teachers to review students' proposals to ensure their relevancy, and in a broader sense, to help the student make successful and lasting edits to the encyclopedia. In doing so, we create a classroom community that enables feedback before students deep dive into the encyclopedia proper. We also provide what we hope is a more welcoming invitation into Wikipedia's complex (and often intimidating) system for the evaluation of sources and content.

What Counts as Knowledge

The past ten years have seen tremendous growth in the adoption of Wikipedia-based educational activities in higher education, in large part due to the consistent efforts of the Wiki Education Foundation. In the social sciences and humanities, many of the instructors engaging Wikipedia-based pedagogies are doing so out of a desire to improve Wikipedia's content gaps, often centered around the gender gap or representation of other marginalized voices.

This emphasis on improving marginalized content in the encyclopedia often leads new editors (students, teachers, and novices, in general) to confront a specific problem related to notability. Marginalization of topics, and the related content gaps, in Wikipedia often comes about due to a kind of societal Catch-22. Articles may be less developed (or non-existent) because there are not enough verifiable secondary sources for Wikipedia editors to draw from. Lack of coverage of a topic in Wikipedia, in this iway, often reflects societal marginalization. When there is little to no secondary coverage of a subject outside of Wikipedia, there's little to draw from to create or add to a parallel article in the encyclopedia.

How Wikipedia decides what counts as "knowledge" through notability teaches students about systemic biases and about the exclusion of marginalized voices. Often students wish to work on topics and people that are of interest to them, yet not enough has been published to meet the requirements of notability, which all but ensures that they need to pick another topic or face deletion.

Who Gets to Contribute

During the multiple conversations we had when writing this book, we often remarked on just how complex Wikipedia has become. The immense bureaucracy of the English language version alone has shown us that it is nearly impossible for any one editor to be completely versed in the numerous policies, guidelines, and unspoken norms that inform editing and interaction. At the same time, we also realized how certain editors in Wikipedia did become extremely literate in their understanding and application of certain policies, especially core policies such as "No Original Research" (WP:NOR). These Wikipedia editors are often those that also act as barriers to students or novices as they use their specialized knowledge.

Learning how to write on Wikipedia for a newcomer can be incredibly frustrating for a variety of reasons, and often results in turning would-be editors away. Wikipedia is incredibly complicated and much more difficult to write than most realize, particularly more difficult than writing essays. Every semester we have taught with Wikipedia, students reflect upon how they did not expect writing on Wikipedia to be so difficult – they not only struggle with sourcing and notability but also with writing neutrality, with organizing their pages properly, and with proper Wiki-style. Without an "assignment" to complete, as well as proper guidance, students often reflect how they would never have taken on such a task.

Beyond the daunting task of "being bold" the immense complexity of Wikipedia acts as a significant barrier to would-be contributors. Despite there being "no firm rules" Wikipedia's policies and guidelines seem nearly limitless to novices, and even to many established Wikipedians. Beyond the tasks of understanding Reliability, Verifiability, Neutrality, and Notability, there are scores of policies and guidelines that govern every detail, and often in slightly contradictory and vague ways that only seasoned Wikipedians can understand and discuss.

Over the years, one of our favorite videos to show students is an Ignite talk from 2010 entitled "Why Wikipedians are the Weirdest people on the Internet" by Steven Walling, where (among other things) he notes that "no one knows what the hell we're saying as we speak a secret jargon filled with over twelve thousand acronyms. No Wikipedian knows them all but we know enough to confuse the hell out of you."[11] While Walling's presentation is ultimately both informative and quite humorous, it illustrates exactly the issue we run into – the barrier to participation is incredibly high for newcomers due to the complexity. Furthermore, those who are able to participate in these conversations on Wikipedia utilize language and knowledge that, intentionally or not, restrict access for those not fluent in "secret jargon."

If all of these barriers to participating were not enough, we have all experienced active gatekeeping from Wikipedians wielding secret jargon and knowledge of obscure and convoluted policies. Whether just "quality snobs" (as Walling notes in his video) or actively prejudiced against students or their topics, some editors have taken it upon themselves to actively lambaste new users' work, or even worse, simply delete it before it has a chance to improve. This can be incredibly discouraging and even disenfranchising to new users and has resulted in numerous long discussions with both students to explain what is going on as well as helpful Wikipedians to help translate and navigate these systems with us.

What we realized through these experiences with newcomers (both in traditional classrooms as well as volunteer settings) is that the frustrations and barriers can be so immense that without a seasoned instructor and mentor, participation on Wikipedia is incredibly unlikely to all but the most diligent. Even with guidance, participation can be difficult and often discouraging, but without active mentorship, editing Wikipedia becomes nearly untenable. The community, while incredibly robust and strong, is not wholly experienced by the new user (especially when only online), and a single negative experience can spoil the potential for new and diverse voices to join the Wikipedia community. In essence, through teaching new users we realized that the complexity of Wikipedia combined with the secret jargon utilized (in combination with those who wield it) actively creates barriers to who contributes, which run counter to the idea of Wikipedia being "the encyclopedia anyone can edit."

How It Actually Works

Knowing all of this, we realized two main things that we wanted to focus on: (1) how Wikipedia works for everyone (how it represents "reality" through its collection of knowledge and distributes it) and (2) how Wikipedia fails to work for everyone (how it excludes certain knowledge and information as well as it has discouraged many potential editors). Our experiences as educators, academics, and volunteers run counter to many of the grand ideas of Wikipedia in relation to what counts as truth, what counts as knowledge, and who gets to contribute. Exploring this became an obsession both personally and professionally, as all of us believed in Wikipedia and its potential – we wanted to "Imagine a world in which every single person on the planet is given free access to the sum of all human knowledge," but to do so required a deeper critique, to ask better questions about, and a fuller exploration of how Wikipedia approached its representation of reality. In the end, this was what inspired this book – our combined love for Wikipedia and our hope to see it constantly improve through engagement, critique, understanding, and most of all, care.

Notes

1 "Edit-a-Thons" are public Wikipedia events, often themed around a topic, that encourage new and established users to write and edit Wikipedia articles, and are led by volunteer instructors.

2 "Wikipedia: Reliable Sources," *Wikipedia*, last modified July 1, 2020, https://en.wikipedia.org/w/index.php?title=Wikipedia:Reliable_sources&oldid=965472450.

3 "Wikipedia: Verifiability," *Wikipedia*, last modified November 29, 2020, https://en.wikipedia.org/w/index.php?title=Wikipedia:Verifiability&oldid=991232984.
4 In Wikipedia, talk pages refer to behind-the-scenes discussion of an article or other page by interested editors.
5 In Wikipedia, mainspace (an abbreviation of "main namespace") refers to the article content that directly covers a topic. The encyclopedia is also made up of a number of other namespaces, such as project space, user space, and talk space, to name a few.
6 Throughout this book, we will use the abbreviated prefix for Wikipedia "WP" when introducing project pages (those that discuss some aspect of Wikipedia policy and are outside mainspace encyclopedic content). For more information about the different spaces in Wikipedia, See Chapter 1.
7 As we discuss in Chapter 1 during the writing of this book the English Wikipedia contained over 6.2 million articles.
8 "Wikipedia: Be Bold," in *Wikipedia*, last modified October 21, 2020, https://en.wikipedia.org/w/index.php?title=Wikipedia:Be_bold&oldid=984736314.
9 On-Wiki, we currently edit and teach under the usernames Matthewvetter and Zach McDowell.
10 "Wikipedia: Be Bold," in *Wikipedia*, last modified October 30, 2001, https://en.wikipedia.org/w/index.php?title=Wikipedia:Be_bold&oldid=238127.
11 *Steven Walling, Why Wikipedians Are the Weirdest People on the Internet*, Ignite Portland, IP8: 2010, https://www.youtube.com/watch?v=UEkF5o6KPNI.

1 Wikipedia's Pillars and the Reality They Construct

> Knowledge about society is thus a realization in the double sense of the word, in the sense of apprehending the objectivated social reality, and in the sense of ongoingly producing this reality.
>
> —Peter L. Berger, *The Social Construction of Reality*

Introduction

A global project, Wikipedia is now both the largest and most widely used encyclopedia in history. As you read this sentence, the encyclopedia "develops at a rate of over 1.9 edits per second, performed by editors from all over the world."[1] As of October 2020, there are currently 55,003,717 articles across more than 270 language versions. The English Wikipedia alone makes up 11% of that total article count, with "6,180,910 articles containing over 3.7 billion words."[2] The English Wikipedia averages over 9 billion page views per month, from over 800 million unique devices. Wikipedia is currently the 13th most visited website globally, and in the US, the 8th most visited.[3] Significantly, only a third of those page views originate in the US, demonstrating the global reach of the English version.[4]

Wikipedia is both an archive and collection of the world's information and history, but also incredibly current and timely. The top-viewed articles tool in the Wikimedia Statistics platform also provides a snapshot of the most topical information. For example, in October 2020 a few of the top-viewed articles included "Ruth Bader Ginsburg," "Amy Coney Barrett," "Shooting of Breonna Taylor," "Dennis Nilsen," and "Joe Biden," as well as entertainment articles on subjects such as "Tenet (film)," "Mulan (2020 film)," and "Cobra Kai."[5] Beyond just archiving history, Wikipedia helps us to understand what the world is thinking about, reading about, and writing about.

DOI: 10.4324/9781003094081-1

For the purpose of this book, we will refer to the English Wikipedia version, given its size and reach, as well as its use of English as international lingua franca. This is not to dismiss the efforts of other Wikipedia projects, but instead to focus on the policies, procedures, and community of the largest Wikipedia project, with hopes that the lessons learned can be translated and applied elsewhere.

As Berger mentions in the epigraph, "knowledge about society is thus a realization in the double sense of the word, in the sense of apprehending the objectivated social reality, and in the sense of ongoingly producing this reality," and if Wikipedia holds the largest knowledge repository, it is imperative to understand how this (social) reality is both apprehended and ongoingly produced on Wikipedia. In this book, we follow the structures of Wikipedia and how the encyclopedia functions to represent "reality" through the collection and dissemination of knowledge. These structures influence policy and guidelines, which then influence community behavior which write, govern, and arbitrate content on Wikipedia. This structure, the fundamental principles of Wikipedia, are known as the "Five Pillars." They act as the basic structure of thinking about what Wikipedia *is* as well as providing a guide to assess how policies, guidelines, and behavior should flow from them, so that the differences between what *should* emerge and what *does not* emerge can be made apparent. In essence, the pillars can act as a baseline to help interpret what happens on Wikipedia, particularly in regard to community behavior and inclusion of content.

Although many in the Wikipedia community have had (and continue conversations) about issues surrounding Wikipedia, this book attempts to bring in others into these complicated discussions through exploring how Wikipedia functions. Wikipedia remains incredibly foreign to many and, despite being ubiquitous, there is a lack of critical engagements with the people, policies, processes, and personalities that govern what is included (and excluded) in Wikipedia outside of the (fairly small and insular) community.

Wikipedia Is *the* Encyclopedia

As the largest and most widely used reference source in history, Wikipedia is the encyclopedia, or as one scholar has called it – the "de facto global reference of dynamic knowledge."[6] For the English-speaking world, this role was formerly held by *Encyclopedia Britannica*, significant as the longest-running print encyclopedia in the English language. Britannica was continuously printed for 244 years. Its final print edition, the 2010 version of the 15th edition, spanned 32 volumes.[7] To give some perspective on the depth and breadth of Wikipedia here, if Wikipedia were printed at the time of this writing, it would span over 2,657 (*Britannica*-sized) volumes.[8] While Britannica continues to be available in the form of an online subscription, Wikipedia's prevalence far eclipses *Britannica's*. In fact, for many secondary and post-secondary students, Wikipedia is the only encyclopedia they have ever known, as an often-quoted 2010 tweet suggests: "Yesterday I asked one of my students if she knew what an encyclopedia is, and she said, Is it something like Wikipedia?"[9]

Millions upon millions of casual users mostly access and know Wikipedia by what the community knows as the "mainspace"[10] – the actual encyclopedia articles, lists, and other "front page" content – with little knowledge of content beyond these pages. In addition to the mainspace, Wikipedia also organizes information into 11 additional namespaces, which include divisions for user pages, files and their metadata, interface texts, templates, help pages, category pages, reader-friendly portals, article drafts, TimedText for media files, and modules. Especially relevant to this investigation is what is known as the "Wikipedia namespace" or "Project namespace." The Project namespace "contains many types of pages connected with the Wikipedia project itself: information, policies, guidelines, essays, processes, discussion, etc."[11] In general, the Project namespace outlines the way in which Wikipedia self-governs. This particular category of information can be identified easily because individual pages will always contain the prefix "Wikipedia:" (which may be abbreviated to "WP:" or "Project"). Throughout this book, we will frequently draw from pages in this namespace to discuss particular policies (e.g., "WP:NPOV" or "Neutral Point of View"), guidelines, or other "meta" information related to the project itself to assess, evaluate, and make sense of how Wikipedia shapes its content, and therefore the representation of reality.

As a whole, this book contends with Wikipedia's dominant status in the global knowledge economy. As the most influential encyclopedia, Wikipedia plays an important role in shaping and arbitrating public knowledge, as well as our epistemological reality (discussed further in this chapter). As we recognize this, however, it's also important to keep in mind that Wikipedia, despite the ways in which it challenges traditional notions of authorship and authority, is part of a long encyclopedic tradition. Such membership is demonstrated to the Wikipedia community and public readership in what is the first among Wikipedia's Five Pillars, the "fundamental principles" describing and governing the encyclopedia. This pillar reads simply: "Wikipedia is an encyclopedia."

Such a statement feels obvious, of course, but bears repeating: "Wikipedia combines many features of generalized and specialized encyclopedias, almanacs, and gazetteers. Wikipedia is not a soapbox, an advertising platform, a vanity press, an experiment in anarchy or democracy, and indiscriminate collection of information, or a web directory."[12] With this statement, the Wikipedia community affirms their project's belonging in a long-standing and distinct written genre, as well as an idea. The encyclopedia is both a space for "the sum of all the world's knowledge," as well a concept more related to its etymology (from Greek *enkyklios paideia*), a "circle of learning."

While reference works akin to encyclopedias have existed long before the first usage of the word encyclopedia, e.g., Pliny's *Natural History* (first century), Vincent de Beauvais' S*peculum Maius* (thirteenth century), the encyclopedic genre as something distinct and encompassing begins to emerge more clearly in Western cultures in and around the Enlightenment period with Francis Bacon's *Novum Organum* (seventeenth century), Denis Diderot and Jean le Rond d'Alembert's *Encyclopédie* (eighteenth century), and *Encyclopædia Britannica* (nineteenth century).[13] By the time Wikipedia came on the scene in the twenty-first century, the genre of the encyclopedia was well-established and already contained specific epistemological assumptions. Foremost among these assumptions is the notion that the collection and curation of human knowledge is even possible, a product perhaps of the scientific rationalism and optimism of the Enlightenment.[14] In fact, if we compare descriptions of Wikipedia with descriptions of one of its Enlightenment-period predecessors, Diderot's *Encyclopédie*, this epistemological assumption is present in both. In 1775, Denis Diderot wrote the following:

> Indeed, the purpose of an encyclopedia is to collect knowledge disseminated around the globe; to set forth its general system to the men with whom we live, and transmit it to those who will come after us, so that the work of preceding centuries will not become useless to the centuries to come; and so that our offspring, becoming better instructed, will at the same time become more virtuous and happy, and that we should not die without having rendered a service to the human race.[15]

Jimmy Wales, who founded Wikipedia as an experimental appendage of *Nupedia*,[16] has explained the project in the following terms: "Imagine a world in which every single person is given free access to the sum of all human knowledge. That's what we're doing."[17] Wales' statement would later become formalized on Wikipedia itself, which now includes the following descriptions of the project: "Wikipedia has a lofty goal: a comprehensive collection of all of the knowledge in the world," along with "Wikipedia's purpose is to benefit the readers by acting as an encyclopedia, a comprehensive written compendium that contains information on all branches of knowledge."[18] Wikipedia's community strives for the incredibly lofty goal of collecting all the knowledge in the world (and distributing it to everyone for free). As becomes apparent in a comparison of these descriptions: the ideological facets of the encyclopedic genre precede and inform Wikipedia, especially in terms of its ambitious goals and lofty rhetoric. Such rhetoric is significant because, as we will explain in the next section (and indeed throughout this book), Wikipedia's epistemological ambition to gather the sum of all human knowledge has specific ontological effects. Achieving (or even attempting) this lofty goal remains incredibly complicated and raises questions around access to knowledge, whose knowledge is included,[19] who contributes, and what counts as knowledge. Wikipedia shapes reality through its representations of the known world, and its curation of the world's knowledge influences particular ways of knowing both information and reality.

Neutrality as the Language of Representation

Wikipedia's capacity to shape reality stems in part from its insistence on neutrality (notably here in lieu of "objectivity" or "truth") in the representation of facts. The encyclopedia's second pillar states that, "Wikipedia is written from a neutral point of view." Wikipedians value and "strive for articles in an impartial tone that document and explain major points of view, giving due weight for their prominence." When a subject is contested, furthermore, Wikipedians "describe multiple points of view, presenting each accurately and in context rather than as 'the truth' or 'the best view.'" Articles should work toward "verifiable accuracy, citing reliable, authoritative sources." Finally, this pillar also firmly recognizes that "editors' personal experiences, interpretations, or opinions do not belong on Wikipedia."[20] Stemming from this second pillar is one of the most fundamental (and earliest) of Wikipedia's major policies: "Neutral Point of View" (WP:NPOV).

Wikipedia's policy article on NPOV lists the following "principles" to ensure that editors "achieve the level of neutrality that is appropriate for the encyclopedia":

- Avoid stating opinions as facts.
- Avoid stating seriously contested assertions as facts.

- Avoid stating facts as opinions.
- Prefer nonjudgmental language.
- Indicate the relative prominence of opposing views.[21]

The emphatic repetition of *fact*, appearing in three of the five principles, is particularly relevant here. In describing policies related to NPOV, Wikipedians are careful to avoid terms such as *objectivity* and *truth*. The community has even acknowledged common challenges and questions related to the policy in a Frequently Asked Questions (FAQ) subpage, identified on that page as an "explanatory supplement."[22] Appearing first on this list is a challenge, "There's no such thing as objectivity," followed-up with a statement and question, "Everybody with any philosophical sophistication knows we all have biases. So, how can we take the NPOV policy seriously?" This probing query is then answered with a clarification regarding the distinction between philosophical objectivity and neutrality as policy that engages description rather than declaration.

> This most common objection to the neutrality policy also reflects the most common *misunderstanding* of the policy. The NPOV policy says nothing about objectivity. In particular, the policy does *not* say that there is such a thing as objectivity in a philosophical sense... such that articles written from that viewpoint are consequently objectively true. That is not the policy, and it is not our aim! Rather, to be neutral is to describe debates rather than engage in them. In other words, when discussing a subject, we should report *what people have said about it* rather than *what is so*.[23]

This accomplishes a kind of side-stepping or substitution for truth or objectivity. In a sense, Wikipedians do not, and do not purport to, declare truth, but instead describe its viewpoints. At the same time, their use of the concept *fact*, which also connotes an empirical objectivity, goes unchallenged. This conceptualization of *fact*, for Wikipedia, is simply "*what people have said*" and relies on secondary sourcing, as Wikipedia summarizes what has already been covered.

Beyond NPOV, Wikipedia's definition of what constitutes a "fact" relies solely on the policy of Verifiability (WP:V), which underscores the encyclopedia's strict adherence to a "no original research" policy in which all content added to mainspace must be verified by any individual encountering that content through a secondary and reliable source. Both policies are discussed at length in Chapter 2 as we demonstrate how Wikipedia has become a trusted and reliable source. So while Wikipedia does not claim to objectively report on truth/s, the encyclopedia does rely on facts, things "actual as opposed to invented,"[24] mediated through a system of policies and processes, and in doing so, actively works toward the construction of reality. In its reliance on "factual" information, Wikipedia not only defines what a fact is (as a verifiable thing that someone has said or published) but also relies on such facts in order to represent and distribute information about our world.

Openness as an Ethic and Ideology

On January 15, 2001, Wikipedia was formally established. A significant day in Internet history, members of the encyclopedia community annually celebrate "Wikipedia day." Furthermore, this day also celebrates when Creative Commons (which developed and continues to develop the open system of copyright Wikipedia employs to ensure it distributes information openly) first registered a website domain.[25] However, Creative Commons history is rooted a bit further than this day of celebration, in an attempt to combat the Sonny Bono Copyright Term Extension Act, enacted in 1998. This act, informally known as the Mickey Mouse Protection Act, added 20 years to the previous 50 years plus life of the creator copyright term.[26] In a lawsuit that eventually found its way to the U.S. Supreme Court, Lawrenge Lessig and Eric Eldred challenged its constitutionality. Although in the end the suit was unsuccessful, it motivated Lessig and others to form Creative Commons as a way to continue Eldred's work "to make more creative works freely available on the internet." The first set of Creative Commons licenses were published in 2002.[27] The founding of Wikipedia and Creative Commons within roughly the same time period points to a larger movement occurring in Internet culture – what might be considered a high water mark of the Free/Libre and Open Source Software (FLOSS) movement.[28] As opposed to proprietary programs or stems, FLOSS (or FOSS) is open source software that "anyone is freely licensed to use, copy, study, and change…in any way."[29]

Among early scholars to theorize Wikipedia's mode of information production, Yochai Benkler recognized Wikipedia as FLOSS due to its radically collaborative methods.[30] But Benkler moved beyond that recognition by also acknowledging Wikipedia as "a core instance of what was emerging as a new mode of production,"[31] what he termed commons-based peer production (or CBPP). CBPP, as Benkler defines it,

> relies on decentralized information gathering and exchange to reduce the uncertainty of participants, and has particular advantages as an information process for identifying human creativity available to work on information and cultural resources in the pursuit of projects, and as an allocation process for allocating that creative effort.[32]

Benkler, along with countless other economic and digital culture theorists that forwarded his work saw a new production value in crowd-sourced projects that were freely open to all to use, modify, and share.

Together, these three contextual factors – a new set of Creative Commons copyright licenses, the FLOSS/FOSS movement, and the emerging theorization of CBPP and crowd-sourcing – best situate Wikipedia's third pillar: "Wikipedia is free content that anyone can use, edit, and distribute." "Since all editors freely license their work to the public," the pillar explains, "no editor owns an article and any contributions can and maybe mercilessly edited and redistributed. Respect copyright laws, and never plagiarize from any sources."[33] In some ways, this third pillar is perhaps the most well-known (though certainly not well-understood) aspect of Wikipedia's culture. Even the most casual reader recognizes Wikipedia as "the free encyclopedia that anyone can edit." In fact, the idea that anyone can edit the encyclopedia has been one of the foremost attributes to be criticized (which we discuss more in Chapter 2). This particular aspect of Wikipedia's free and open culture has become both an ethic and ideology. As an ethical stance, Wikipedia's free culture creates positive associations related to democratic and participatory methods and knowledge equity (the notion that knowledge and information should be free). Ideologically, Wikipedia's free culture stands in opposition to proprietary and market-driven systems. As Benkler notes, in the case of Wikipedia:

> Neither state administration nor corporate managerial hierarchy was necessary for groups to scale to large numbers and effectively produce critical information, knowledge, and cultural goods.... We can think of it as freedom from hierarchy or domination [in addition to] freedom from markets.[34]

The Wiki platform itself, which encourages collaboration, development, and networking, was much celebrated in the 1990s and early aughts as a platform that would lead to both increased participation and diversity of participation in FLOSS and FOSS projects.[35] The term "Wiki" was introduced by Ward Cunningham in 1995 with WikiWikiWeb (WikiWiki means "fast" or "hurry" in Hawaiian).[36] Wikis allow anyone to contribute in a distributed manner and harness the link-ability of Internet pages (blue links, on Wikipedia, for example, that link to other Wikipedia pages, defining and covering other topics, concepts, and people), allowing for a linked collaborative space which can be contributed to, accessed by, and shared with anyone with access to the Internet.[37] When paired with the ideologies of openness and knowledge sharing, the Wiki platform became tremendously successful enabling Wikipedia's growth, as well as many other Wiki-based projects.

For Wikipedia, the work of the concept "free" – both in terms of its ethical and ideological associations – has been incredibly productive. The Wikipedia idea has captured and continues to capture the imaginations of thousands of volunteers. Its growth and size, which we highlighted in the introduction to this chapter, was both previously unimagined and unprecedented. We see Wikipedia's success as at least partially due to the (techno)optimistic rhetoric that accompanied it. Like most (techno)optimism of the early 2000s, however, Wikipedia's rhetoric was overly ambitious and somewhat naive.

The encyclopedia that "anyone can edit," as it turns out, is mostly edited by male contributors. As Heather Ford and Judy Wajcman write: "While exact numbers are difficult to estimate, no one disputes that the overwhelming majority of contributors are male."[38] This leads to a fairly unbalanced editorship, which leads to unbalanced coverage and inclusion of people and topics. For example, there is a significant lack of coverage of women on Wikipedia, as only 17% of the bibliographic articles on the English Wikipedia are on women.[39]

Wikipedia's gender gap, as it has come to be known, is understood as a direct result of this homogenous editorship and the resulting gaps in representation, especially when it comes to the representation of women and women's issues. While other gaps have been identified and discussed, the systemic biases surrounding gender in Wikipedia continue to be the most well-known. But all of these biases present a challenge to the optimistic and ambitious rhetoric related to Wikipedia's free and open culture. Even in the most well-established and developed language version (English), and even after 20 years of development, Wikipedia has not completely fulfilled its mission of openness.

The lack of diversity in its editor demographic especially has limited the encyclopedia's ability to fully harness the power of the participatory platform and ethic. In addition to issues related to systemic biases, discussed in Chapter 3 (as well as throughout the book), Wikipedia has also faced challenges related to information access. The encyclopedia attempts to gather and make free and open the world's knowledge, yet much of this knowledge is behind paywalls, or other barriers to open access. While the Wikipedia community has started initiatives like 1Lib1Ref (short for one librarian, one reference), a campaign that invites librarians (who would have access to paywalled sources) to improve articles by adding citations, information access continues to be a major barrier to improving knowledge equity.[40]

Despite its success, the encyclopedia still has a long way to go in terms of encouraging diversity of participation and knowledge equity, which we discuss further in Chapters 4 and 5. By attending to Wikipedia's shortcomings in a more nuanced exploration of the community and its policies, this book seeks to advocate for an increased understanding of Wikipedia's attention to openness, and create a better space to hold better conversations about its future.

Wikipedia Is a Community

The fourth pillar, "Wikipedia's editors should treat each other with respect and civility," seems fairly straightforward at first, but reveals something fundamental about Wikipedia that many do not consider when thinking about Wikipedia: Wikipedia is a community. Along with Wikipedia's lofty goals, enormous collection of content, and rather large foundation backing it, Wikipedia has always been a community of individuals with the shared goal of collecting and sharing the world's knowledge. Rather than simply approaching Wikipedia as a "site" or even a repository of knowledge, Wikipedia must also be approached and understood as a community, one with all the eccentricities and flaws that accompany any community (particularly one on the Internet focused on producing a general knowledge encyclopedia). Policies and procedures are enacted and created by the community, and in the end, it is the community that shapes Wikipedia, and therefore the representation of reality.

At a fundamental level, the fourth pillar asks editors to be nice to each other, but it is a rather vague statement with lofty intentions. Numerous community guidelines and policies have emerged from this pillar to lay out behavioral expectations and interaction policies. The guideline "Please don't bite the newcomers" (WP:BITE) is a prime example of a guideline that emerged from this pillar, as it encourages users to be kind to new participants, hoping not to scare them off.[41] This guideline is both indicative of how the community utilizes guidelines to encourage behavior as well as indicative of exactly why these guidelines are necessary: Wikipedia, like many other online spaces, is often viewed as unwelcoming to new users. With a community as complicated and with as many guidelines and rules as Wikipedia has, it is often difficult for new users to get involved, and without gentle, caring guidance from seasoned veterans, new users often get discouraged or simply stop participating. This becomes even more troubling when considering Wikipedia's editor demographic and the resulting issues related to gender.

Setting aside the issue of demographics, the fundamental structure of Wikipedia is to represent secondary information, which already creates issues of inclusion issues due to systemic biases. Wikipedia's community makeup obviously only further elevates these concerns. Exploring these tensions between the way that Wikipedia functions to include (and exclude) information and how the community participates in alleviating (or aggravating) issues of inclusion and representation is fundamental to understanding who and what "counts" as knowledge on Wikipedia.

As part of this enquiry, we will explore the tensions between the intentions of the community (and the policies and guidelines that emerged from the community), some of the concerns and issues that have emerged from these tensions, and how the community has addressed and continues to address these issues. Many in the community (as well as the Wikimedia Foundation more broadly) have recognized a need to change and evolve. Part of a series of policy initiatives that emerged from the "Wikimedia 2030" community conversations that attempt to visualize what the Wikimedia projects, and Wikipedia, in particular, should encompass and represent in the future, the development of a "Universal Code of Conduct" attempts to "Provide for Safety and Inclusion" by explicitly stating behavior guidelines for community members.[42] This, amongst other initiatives we will discuss further throughout the book, but particularly in Chapter 5, are ways that the community has begun to work on addressing a number of issues with Wikipedia and the community.

Wikipedia Has No Firm Rules

Although Wikipedia explicitly states that it is not an "anarchy," "democracy," or "bureaucracy," the style of consensus-based decision-making that Wikipedia utilizes to create policies, guidelines, and other community decisions is complicated, messy, and (fairly) radical.[43] The fifth pillar of Wikipedia, "Wikipedia has no firm rules," speaks to the ability of the community to shape the rules of Wikipedia as it sees fit to best achieve the goals of the encyclopedia. Not only is Wikipedia *the* encyclopedia and *the* place where much of the world obtains information, but the community of Wikipedia defines *how*, on a micro level, Wikipedia obtains, collects, and distributes information and knowledge. Each policy and guideline has the ability to change and evolve (and has) over time. Despite there being "no firm rules," Wikipedia has hundreds of guidelines and policies to help govern and get a handle on the chaotic and infinite task of collecting and distributing the world's knowledge. Each one of these policies and guidelines influence how and why certain topics and people are included or excluded. Through this influence, Wikipedia is shaped, and then therefore shapes not only the body of knowledge that is collected but also it shapes how the information is represented. The "rules" of Wikipedia, therefore (firm or not) shape the representation of information, and therefore the representation of the reality of what exists is important, and is available for consumption.

No Rules, But Lots of Hierarchy

Slightly contrary to the slogan "the encyclopedia anyone can edit," Wikipedia actually employs a fairly robust hierarchy of rules and protections, many which remain imperative to combatting the "firehose of misinformation" that inevitably flows freely when "anyone can edit." Many tasks, including creating new pages or even editing privileges on some pages (particularly controversial ones or of famous people especially) are "protected" from editors without advanced permissions.

Along with the hundreds of policies and guidelines, Wikipedia, much like many online communities, utilizes a system of user access levels to manage these permissions. User access levels define editors' permissions or "abilities to perform specific actions on Wikipedia."[44] While any user, regardless of being logged into a registered account, can view and edit many articles, additional specialized permissions become available to registered users, particularly articles with a long history of fame or controversy.

Wikipedia has six levels of user access levels, four of which are automatically assigned utilizing participation levels and time, while two are conferred upon users through community consensus. First, unregistered users consist of users that are not logged in. Unless their IP address has been blocked for a previous editorial action, unregistered users may edit pages that are not protected. Like all edits, edits are recorded in history pages, but are listed by the IP address. Likewise, registered (new) users may make edits to pages that are not protected or semi-protected, but they cannot create, move, or rename pages. This user group is also restricted from uploading images or other files. Newly registered users can edit preferences, create a user page, and their history of contributions is recorded in association with their username, which allows them to build up time and edit history to become autoconfirmed and confirmed users. Newly registered users whose accounts are "at least 4 days old and who have made at least 10 edits" automatically are added to the group. These users can create new Wikipedia articles, move pages, edit semi-protected pages, and upload files. As of February 2019, there were 1.7 million confirmed users "of which the vast majority were inactive."[45] Editors can additionally become "extended confirmed" when their account is at least 30 days old and they have made at least 500 edits. These users can edit pages locked "under extended confirmed protection" – a more secure level of protection. As of October 2020, there are 52,988 users identified as "extended confirmed."[46] These access levels are all usually conferred automatically (or if an administrator "confirms" the user manually).

The two highest user access levels conferred on Wikipedia, administrators and bureaucrats, are approved through community consensus. Both of these involve "in-depth and considerable discussion and examination of the candidate's activity and contributions as an editor."[47] Administrators can access tools and abilities such as "page deletion, page protection, blocking and unblocking users, and the ability to edit full protected pages," as well as "grant and remove most access rights to other users." Bureaucrats can also grant and remove administrator access.[48] However, these users do not have more power or control when it comes to article content. Finally, as with all editors, none of these users are employed in their user roles by the Wikimedia foundation, the organization that runs Wikipedia. All of these roles, even the administration and bureaucrat roles, are volunteer only.

Wikipedia as Cultural Hegemony

To understand the importance of why Wikipedia is so pivotal, and how its policies, guidelines, and community influence (through the encyclopedia) how knowledge (and therefore reality itself) is represented, it is imperative to understand how information representation can influence culture and ideology.

Since Wikipedia is one of the largest repositories for information in the world, and one of the top sites to access information from, Wikipedia acts as part of a "cultural hegemony" as those who access it participate in the outcome of Wikipedia's policies and guidelines. Wikipedia's policies and guidelines become more than just ways to control the encyclopedia, and instead become what Antonio Gramsci calls "cultural hegemony" – the beliefs and powers that control the norms of society.[49] Wikipedia participates, mirrors, and amplifies cultural hegemony, particularly in the English Wikipedia (the lingua franca of cultural hegemony to begin with). The guidelines and policies of Wikipedia and how they are put into practice are ideological in nature, as they govern how information can be represented. Furthermore, participating in Wikipedia, whether actively editing or reading, acts as participation in this hegemonic power. Users actively consent to this representation, this ideology, without knowing how it forms understandings of how information is represented. The system of ideas and ideals that govern representation on Wikipedia is hidden beneath the consciousness of the consumers of the encyclopedia. As Marx notes of ideology (as it relates to labor and value), "they do not know it, but they do it."[50] Furthermore, for general readers, Wikipedia's project to enable free access to the sum of all human knowledge not only creates the conditions in which the sum of all human knowledge is represented (i.e., Western logocentrism) but also operates as a stand-in, an effective synecdoche, for the representation of all human knowledge. This all being said, despite Wikipedia's incompleteness and despite its systemic biases, we (and many others) believe that Wikipedia still serves as the best option we have for representing human knowledge, and therefore must be understood, analyzed, and improved to work toward this grand goal. As *the* encyclopedia, Wikipedia shapes how we access knowledge and what knowledge we have access to, and that remains imperative to understanding our present and future.

An archaeological Approach to Wikipedia

As a repository of global knowledge, Wikipedia certainly offers us a glimpse of how certain epistemologies control and shape information. But how does Wikipedia shape reality? How does an encyclopedia have an ontological impact on those that interact with it?

We make this argument in two distinct parts. First, in shaping our perception and understanding of the world around us, Wikipedia creates an epistemological reality. Many of the concepts, places, people, and events (all of the material and immaterial, abstract, and concrete objects of our everyday experience) are covered and reiterated through Wikipedia's representations. Mark Graham, in "Wiki Space: Palimpsests and the Politics of Exclusion," applies this process to understanding interaction with place, as he argues that "how places are represented and made visible (or invisible) in Wikipedia has a potentially immense bearing on the ways that people interact with those same places culturally, economically, and politically."[51] "Because Wikipedia is now a de facto global reference of dynamic knowledge," Graham continues, "spatial representations distributed throughout [the encyclopedia] thus ultimately become a performative media embedded into the myriad decisions made by hundreds of millions of users."[52] Throughout this book, we extend the work of Graham, arguing that epistemological constructions in Wikipedia apply to more than spatial geographies, but in representations of all manner of things, both through inclusive acts as well as exclusionary practices (more on that in Chapter 3).

Second, we also contend that the ways in which users of Wikipedia *interact* with the encyclopedia also have implications for how users understand knowledge systems, in general, as well as understanding the behaviors of those involved in the knowledge production. From everyday readers who passively consume information, critically or uncritically, without much participation beyond that – to more active editors who contribute to the encyclopedia in a diversity of ways: the ways in which users engage the encyclopedia, whether for consumption, production, or even critique, have implications for understanding the ways in which they engage the larger information ecology. Quite specifically, it is evidenced that users that can understand and enter into discourse related to processes for evaluation in Wikipedia may also be more likely to critically evaluate other media platforms.[53,54] The ways in which Wikipedia function as a space in which the users *being* is shaped here emerge in multiple ways here, not only defining what is reliable, notable, available, and accessible but also shaping information literacy skills, informing agency around knowledge production. In short, Wikipedia functions as a space that not only defines the boundaries of "what is knowable" (what is knowledge) but also shapes "how we know" through the ways in which it allows the collection and distribution of knowledge. All of this emerges through the complex ways in which Wikipedia functions both as an encyclopedia and as a community.

Instead of simply analyzing policy, this book examines the construction of the encyclopedia through its policies, community, and site itself (the "medium" of Wikipedia, which is also a function of its policies and community, of course). We examine how Wikipedia's policies and guidelines are enacted and changed, as well as how Wikipedia's content remains governed by powers and people's actions that exist beyond and outside of policies. Much of how Wikipedia functions is "hidden" either subconsciously by the individuals or beyond the reach of a straightforward policy analysis. There are things that happen in and on Wikipedia that are not recorded or stated, yet have enormous power. We examine these discursive formations on Wikipedia as governed by rules beyond those of grammar and logic that (often) operate beneath the consciousness of individual subjects. Beyond analyzing policy, we approach Wikipedia somewhat archaeologically (in a Foucauldian sense) as Wikipedia functions utilizing "hidden" systems of conditions and relations that influence discursive practices.[55] Foucault referred to the extraction and understanding of these rules to help illuminate the unsaid and hidden system, which helps shine light on how the systems actually function. On Wikipedia, there are plenty of written rules that govern how information should be represented, what grammar and logical systems should be employed, and what should be included – there are literally hundreds of rules and guidelines that pertain to various aspects of Wikipedia's editorial governance. However, there is a gap between what is in the guidelines and rules, and what is actually implemented. There is vagueness to these policies and practices that opens a space for the un-said, the unwritten, and the "rules" that exist beneath and before those of the discursive practices of Wikipedia.

To understand this gap, we invoke Steven Thorne's concept "culture-of-use." Thorne's theory can be applied to any kind of digital communication technology or tool in order to understand how "linguistic, multimodal, cultural, interactional, and cognitive practices" emerge "in the articulation between the immediate contextual aspects of the communicative event at hand and the historically sedimented associations, purposes, and values that accrue to a digital communication tool from its everyday use."[56] The idea that wikis (as networked software platform) and Wikipedia, as a particular application of the wiki, gather "historically sedimented characteristics" underscores the necessity for an archeological approach. As we excavate Wikipedia's often unspoken archaeology, we also attend to how the encyclopedia has developed a certain culture that originated in (1) a very homogenous demographic of highly educated, white, and male participants, at a time when (2) the early web promised an overly optimistic, and even emancipatory, democratization of knowledge and participation.

Of course, this endeavor is not just about the history of Wikipedia. As Jussi Parikka reminds us, "archaeology is always, implicitly or explicitly, about the present: what is our present moment in its objects, discourses and practices, and how did it become to be perceived as *reality*"[57] (emphasis ours). Reading the representation of reality through these unwritten rules is tricky, as it requires understanding both how the rules and guidelines themselves function, and how parts of the system of rules and guidelines open up space for the unwritten. Rather than simply tracing what is *written* or *said* to be a rule or guideline, instead what we lay out is what actually *happens* on Wikipedia through both the rules that are stated, and the practices that evolve with and between those rules, and investigate the various power systems and decisions that may influence the actual outcomes. To put these systems and their outcomes in another context, Alexander Galloway maintains that computerized systems, particularly as they relate to digital media platforms that host information, contain "an ethic." Platforms such as Wikipedia "do" things (they shape outcomes, control inclusion and exclusion) and are representative of that ethic.[58] So one of the ways we can think about the "archaeology" of Wikipedia here is to read the "ethics" of Wikipedia – not about good or bad (although there are plenty of areas to infer these types of judgments) but what are the "ethics" that we can read through what Wikipedia "*does*" *to*, *with*, and *for* information representation?

We explore these ethics through a series of policies and guidelines on Wikipedia, moving beyond what is simply stated, and instead approach how these policies and guidelines are implemented in the construction of the largest repository of knowledge in history. Evaluating the "ethics" of Wikipedia beyond what the stated goals are (and possibly antithetical to these goals) helps to enlighten the overall ways in which Wikipedia's reality is represented, and the possible concerns and outcomes for the "ethical" reality. Throughout this book, turn to and explore how the community implements rules in various ways that help to shed light on these "ethics" that shape Wikipedia.

In the pursuit of deriving a critical understanding of the inner workings of Wikipedia, we focus on three major areas in which it shapes its content. First, through an analysis of how Wikipedia constructs reliability we explore the rules and procedures under how Wikipedia defines what counts as true and reliable for inclusion into Wikipedia. Second, we analyze the policies and procedures for what Wikipedia allows for inclusion into the encyclopedia, as well as how it defines itself through exclusion. Third, we dive into how the community interacts and welcomes (or excludes) participation, and how this shapes what is possible on and for Wikipedia. Through these analyses and expositions, we bring these findings and observations together to understand the bigger picture of how, beyond what is evident in policies, procedures, and community outreach, Wikipedia functions (for better or worse) to shape the information repository which then shapes our reality. Exposing these innerworkings allows us to establish not only a more rigorous critique of this incredibly important system, but we also will offer some insights into how to engage and improve the ways in which we shape reality (together).

Notes

1 Wikipedia, s.v. "Wikipedia:Statistics," last modified October 3, 2020, https://en.wikipedia.org/w/index.php?title=Wikipedia:Statistics&oldid=981585678.
2 Ibid.
3 "Wikipedia.Org Competitive Analysis, Marketing Mix and Traffic – Alexa," last modified January 5, 2021, https://www.alexa.com/siteinfo/wikipedia.org.
4 "Wikistats – Statistics For Wikimedia Projects," last modified January 5, 2021, https://stats.wikimedia.org/#/en.wikipedia.org.
5 Ibid.
6 Mark Graham, "Wiki Space: Palimpsests and the Politics of Exclusion," in *Critical Point of View: A Wikipedia Reader*, eds. Geert Lovink and Nathaniel Tkacz (Amsterdam: Institute of Network Cultures, 2011), 269.
7 "Encyclopædia Britannica," Wikipedia, last modified December 20, 2020, https://en.wikipedia.org/w/index.php?title=Encyclop%C3%A6dia_Britannica&oldid=995346575.
8 "Wikipedia:Size of Wikipedia," Wikipedia, last modified December 25, 2020, https://en.wikipedia.org/w/index.php?title=Wikipedia:Size_of_Wikipedia&oldid=996199067.
9 Alison Clement, Twitter Post, January 30, 2010, 2:00 p.m, https://twitter.com/alisonclement/status/8421314259.
10 Wikipedia technically calls it "main namespace," however it is most often referred to as "mainspace" throughout the Wikipedia community. We will utilize this term throughout to refer to the parts of Wikipedia that contain the encyclopedic content, in contrast with the "Project namespace" pages (or "Wikipedia namespace") that contain policies and guidelines that we will also often refer to.
11 "Wikipedia:Namespace," Wikipedia, last modified December 22, 2020, https://en.wikipedia.org/w/index.php?title=Wikipedia:Namespace&oldid=995798895.
12 "Wikipedia:Five Pillars," Wikipedia, last modified December 27, 2020, https://en.wikipedia.org/w/index.php?title=Wikipedia:Five_pillars&oldid=996637443.
13 Dan O'Sullivan, "What Is an Encyclopedia? A Brief Overview from Pliny to Wikipedia," in *Critical Point of View: A Wikipedia Reader*, eds. Geert Lovink and Nathaniel Tkacz (Amsterdam: Institute of Network Cultures, 2011), 34–49.

14 Matthew A. Vetter, "Possible Enlightenments: Wikipedia's Encyclopedic Promise and Epistemological Failure," in *Wikipedia @ 20: Stories of an Incomplete Revolution*, eds. Joseph Reagle and Jackie Koerner (Cambridge, MA: MIT Press, 2020), 285–295.
15 Denis Diderot, "Encyclopedia," *The Encyclopedia of Diderot & d'Alembert Collaborative Translation Project*, trans. Philip Stewart (Ann Arbor: Michigan Publishing, University of Michigan Library, 2002), accessed January 5, 2020, http://hdl.handle.net/2027/spo.did2222.0000.004. Originally published as "Encyclopédie," *Encyclopédie ou Dictionnaire raisonné des sciences, des arts et des métiers*, 5: 635–648A (Paris, 1755).
16 For further explanation of Wikipedia's origins, see Andrew Lih, *The Wikipedia Revolution: How a Bunch of Nobodies Created the World's Greatest Encyclopedia*, 1st ed. (New York: Hyperion, 2009).
17 Roblimo, "Wikipedia Founder Jimmy Wales Responds," *Slashdot* (blog), July 28, 2004, https://slashdot.org/story/04/07/28/1351230/wikipedia-founder-jimmy-wales-responds.
18 "Wikipedia:Purpose," Wikipedia, last modified December 15, 2020, https://en.wikipedia.org/w/index.php?title=Wikipedia:Purpose&oldid=994329979.
19 Also the name of an initiative to address knowledge and inclusion gaps on Wikipedia. More information at https://whoseknowledge.org/.
20 "Wikipedia:Five Pillars," Wikipedia, last modified December 27, 2020, https://en.wikipedia.org/w/index.php?title=Wikipedia:Five_pillars&oldid=996637443.
21 "Wikipedia:Neutral Point of View," Wikipedia, November 10, 2001. https://en.wikipedia.org/w/index.php?title=Wikipedia:Neutral_point_of_view&oldid=334854039.
22 "Wikipedia:Neutral Point of View/FAQ," Wikipedia, last modified December 29, 2020, https://en.wikipedia.org/w/index.php?title=Wikipedia:Neutral_point_of_view/FAQ&oldid=996952192.
23 Ibid.
24 "Fact," Wiktionary: The Free Dictionary, accessed December 29, 2020. https://en.wiktionary.org/wiki/fact.
25 "Wikipedia:Wikipedia Day," Wikipedia, last modified November 25, 2020, https://en.wikipedia.org/w/index.php?title=Wikipedia:Wikipedia_Day&oldid=990613284.
26 Creative Commons, "The Story of Creative Commons," accessed December 30, 2020, https://certificates.creativecommons.org/cccertedu/chapter/1-1-the-story-of-creative-commons/.
27 Ibid.
28 For more on the history of F.O.S.S. movements, see "History of Free and Open-Source Software," Wikipedia, last modified December 1, 2020, https://en.wikipedia.org/w/index.php?title=History_of_free_and_open-source_software&oldid=991662037.
29 "Free and Open-Source Software," Wikipedia, last modified December 25, 2020, https://en.wikipedia.org/w/index.php?title=Free_and_open-source_software&oldid=996259231.
30 Yochai Benkler, "Coase's Penguin, or, Linux and 'The Nature of the Firm,'" *The Yale Law Journal* 112, no. 3 (2002): 369–446. https://doi.org/10.2307/1562247.

31 Yochai Benkler, "From Utopia to Practice and Back," in *Wikipedia @ 20: Stories of an Incomplete Revolution*, (Cambridge, MA: MIT Press, 2020).
32 Benkler, "Coase's Penguin."
33 "Wikipedia:Five Pillars," Wikipedia, last modified December 27, 2020, https://en.wikipedia.org/w/index.php?title=Wikipedia:Five_pillars&oldid=996637443.
34 Benkler, "From Utopia," 45.
35 Yochai Benkler, "Coase's Penguin."
36 Ward Cunningham, WikiWikiWeb (web page), accessed January 6, 2021, https://wiki.c2.com/.
37 Bo Leuf and Ward Cunningham, *The Wiki Way: Quick Collaboration on the Web* (Boston: Addison-Wesley, 2001).
38 Heather Ford and Judy Wajcman, "'Anyone Can Edit', Not Everyone Does: Wikipedia's Infrastructure and the Gender Gap," *Social Studies of Science* 47, no. 4 (August 1, 2017): 511–527. https://doi.org/10.1177/03063127 17692172.
39 "Gender by Wikipedia Language," Wikipedia Human Gender Indicators, June 9, 2015, https://whgi.wmflabs.org/gender-by-language.html.
40 "1Lib1Ref," Wikipedia, last modified November 2, 2020, https://en.wikipedia.org/w/index.php?title=1Lib1Ref&oldid=986673021.
41 "Wikipedia: Please Do Not Bite the Newcomers," Wikipedia, last modified December 22, 2020, https://en.wikipedia.org/w/index.php?title=Wikipedia:Please_do_not_bite_the_newcomers&oldid=995712413.
42 "Universal Code of Conduct – Meta," Wikimedia, last modified January 6, 2021, https://meta.wikimedia.org/w/index.php?title=Universal_Code_of_Conduct&oldid=20931352.
43 "Wikipedia: What Wikipedia Is Not," Wikipedia, last modified July 15, 2020, https://en.wikipedia.org/w/index.php?title=Wikipedia:What_Wikipedia_is_not&oldid=967817887.
44 "Wikipedia: User Access Levels," Wikipedia, last modified January 1, 2021, https://en.wikipedia.org/w/index.php?title=Wikipedia:User_access_levels&oldid=997595794.
45 Ibid.
46 Ibid.
47 Ibid.
48 Ibid.
49 For more on this, see Raymond Williams, *Marxism and Literature* (Oxford: Oxford University Press, 1977), and Antonio Gramsci, *Selections from the Prison Notebooks of Antonio Gramsc*i. Edited and translated by Quintin Hoare and Geoffrey Nowell Smith (London: Lawrence and Wishart, 1971).
50 Karl Marx. 1996. *Das Kapita*l. Edited by Friedrich Engels. Washington, D.C.: Regnery Publishing.
51 Graham, "Wiki Space," 269.
52 Ibid.
53 Zachary J. McDowell and Matthew A. Vetter, "It Takes a Village to Combat a Fake News Army: Wikipedia's Community and Policies for Information Literacy," *Social Media + Society* 6, no. 3 (July 1, 2020): https://doi.org/10.1177/2056305120937309.

54 Matthew A. Vetter, Zachary J. McDowell, and Mahala Stewart, "From Opportunities to Outcomes: The Wikipedia-Based Writing Assignment," *Computers and Composition* 52 (June 1, 2019): 53–64. https://doi.org/10.1016/j.compcom.2019.01.008.

55 Michel Foucault, *The Archaeology of Knowledge & The Discourse on Language* (New York: Vintage, 1982).

56 Steven L. Thorne, "Cultures-of-use and Morphologies of Communicative Action. Language Learning & Technology," 20, no. 2 (2016): 185, http://llt.msu.edu/issues/june 2016/thorne.pdf

57 Jussi Parikka, *What Is Media Archaeology?* (Cambridge, UK ; Malden, MA: Polity, 2012).

58 Alexander R. Galloway, *The Interface Effect* (Cambridge, UK ; Malden, MA: Polity, 2012).

2 What Counts as Information

The Construction of Reliability and Verifiability

> A few endorse Wikipedia heartily. This mystifies me. Education is not a matter of popularity or of convenience—it is a matter of learning, of knowledge gained the hard way, and of respect for the human record. A professor who encourages the use of Wikipedia is the intellectual equivalent of a dietician who recommends a steady diet of Big Macs with everything.
>
> —Michael Gorman, former president of ALA, 2007

Introduction

In Chapter 1, we introduced the argument that Wikipedia functions to represent reality through the collection and dissemination of knowledge. In our review of the encyclopedia's five pillars, the encyclopedia's fundamental principles, we began a discussion regarding Wikipedia's ideals and what emerges in actual practice. This chapter continues that discussion by focusing on policies stemming from the second pillar: "Wikipedia is written from a neutral point of view." While Chapter 1 sought to explain how Wikipedia constructs its reality, this chapter addresses how the encyclopedia constructs what counts as information, or what the community calls reliability and verifiability.

The epigraph above harkens back to Wikipedia's early days. In 2007, Wikipedia turned six years old. During this period, the encyclopedia experienced both its most dramatic growth and its most widespread criticism. At the beginning of 2004 the English Wikipedia[1] contained a mere 188,000 articles, by 2007 the encyclopedia boasted 1,560,000 mainspace articles, and in two years, by 2009, it had nearly doubled to 2,679,000.[2] Such rapid growth, when combined with the encyclopedia's rising popularity, inspired the wrath of more than a few critics, often academics or public intellectuals, to publicly lambaste the project. For instance, in June of 2007, Michael Gorman, former president of the

DOI: 10.4324/9781003094081-2

American Library Association (ALA), forwarding a larger critique of the disastrous impact of digital technologies on learning, published "Jabberwiki: The Educational Response, Part II."[3] The brief essay appeared in an *Encyclopedia Britannica* blog, as part of a larger forum comprising editorials on the topic of Web 2.0.

Immediately preceding the statements shared in the epigraph above, Gorman cast doubt on the crowd-sourced model of Wikipedia, urging his readers to question two specific facets of the encyclopedia's construction: "first that an authoritative work can be the result of the aggregation of the opinions of self-selected anonymous 'experts' with or without credentials and, second, that the collective wisdom of the cyberswarm will correct errors and ensure authority."[4] Gorman's critiques were typical of the time, as few understood how the encyclopedia functioned, especially as he seemed to believe that an "aggregation" of "opinions" was what constituted Wikipedia.

What Gorman failed to consider was the multitude of policies and guidelines that had already been developed to protect against misinformation as well as errors related to his critiques. One of the earliest policies, "Neutral Point of View" (WP:NPOV, or just NPOV), existed as early as 2001, and actively guards against the insertion of opinions in Wikipedia.[5] Furthermore, "Verifiability" (WP:V) which was formalized by 2003, similarly, ensures that encyclopedic content can be validated and corrected when editors verify a source (along with any edits made from that particular source) requiring that content on Wikipedia comes from a reputable, verifiable, secondary source.[6] Taken together, Gorman's critiques of Wikipedia were misinformed (especially in 2007) as Wikipedia specifically utilized reputable and credentialed sources to build mainspace articles. Now in its twentieth year (at the time of this writing), Wikipedia has matured into the "Internet's good grown-up," a community that "exists to battle fake news," and "the last best place on the Internet."[7] Preceding this new reputation, numerous studies have favorably compared Wikipedia's accuracy to "traditional" encyclopedias.[8] How did Wikipedia get here? Through an exploration of the overt policies and behind-the-scenes practices we can trace how Wikipedia has emerged as a reliable source in an age of misinformation.

Problematic Information

To better understand Wikipedia's place in the digital information ecology, a brief review of issues surrounding contemporary understandings of "problematic information" is particularly useful. Terms like *fake news*, *misinformation*, and *disinformation*, although frequently used in both public and specialized discourse, are slippery, each with multiple competing associations and connotations. Further exploring the classificatory work by Caroline Jack, *Lexicon of Lies: Terms for Problematic Information*, through connecting her taxonomy of problematic information to terms and policies employed in Wikipedia, we can help illuminate the construction and role of reliability on the encyclopedia.[9] Misinformation and disinformation are both types of problematic information, with a difference of intent. Misinformation includes "information whose inaccuracy is unintentional" whereas disinformation is "deliberately false or misleading."[10]

The crisis of "problematic information," what Jack defines as "inaccurate, misleading, inappropriately attributed, or altogether fabricated"[11] information, points to a set of circumstances in which media ecologies fail to address challenges pertaining to authenticity, rhetorical manipulation, and the inability of educational institutions to adequately teach critical media literacy. While popular social media sites such as Facebook are most often cited as helping spread problematic information, no socially driven media is completely unscathed.

While Wikipedia is not completely immune to problematic information in the form of propaganda, information policies surrounding Conflict of Interest (CoI) often deter types of political mis/disinformation. Jowett and O'Donnell distinguish between white, black, and grey types of propaganda to differentiate between accurate but selectively presented or cherry-picked information (white); blatant inaccurate or deceptive information (black); or some combination of both (grey).[12] In the midst of the current infodemic, the encyclopedia has been recognized as an essential resource for accurate public health information related to COVID-19.[13] In fact, at the time of writing, over 87,000 volunteer editors have created and maintained more than 5,200 Wikipedia articles which have been viewed more than 532 million times.[14]

An Assemblage of Policies

Wikipedia employs community-mediated information policies to construct reliability, and guard against a number of types of problematic information. Defining reliability as an enacted and experiential program assembled by multiple social actors, policies, and algorithmic processes, we employ the term ethical assemblage as a shorthand for the process for which the construction of reliability occurs (which in turn has led to the credibility of Wikipedia). We invoke the term assemblage in the tradition of Deleuze and Parnet, as well as scholars influenced by the material and ecological implications of their work in rhetoric and media studies.[15] For Deleuze and Parnet, an assemblage is "a multiplicity which is made up of many heterogeneous terms and which establishes liaisons, relations between them across ages, sexes and reigns—different natures."[16] In our application of assemblage to Wikipedia's information processes, we read socio-material assemblages as dispersed textualities and agents that work to co-construct reliability within the encyclopedia. Such assemblages include policy (i.e., neutrality, verifiability) and policy enactments (the broad application of policy to editorial processes throughout the encyclopedia), but also involve other human and non-human agents in the co-construction of reliability.[17] Considering this co-construction as an assemblage helps to underscore a major aspect of these policies, enactments, and other agents – they are not only co-constructing reliability but each of the aspects are also interrelated. Policies and guidelines reference each other in a web of interdependence, the community both enacts policies and guidelines as well as makes decisions about and authors policies and guidelines, and software and automated aspects of Wikipedia function within this system. Each piece of the system is important to consider, but they are never alone or individual as the interdependence and interaction between all of these aspects is the key to understanding how Wikipedia constructs reliability. In summary, to understand reliability on Wikipedia we must illustrate each of these aspects, but also pay close attention to how they function together as an assemblage, as this is how we understand the ethic (what the computerized system does) of reliability on Wikipedia.

This section is an effort to further elucidate the policies of NPOV and Verifiability, as well as those adjacent to them, to elucidate how they work toward the construction of reliability on Wikipedia. Through reviewing Wikipedia definitions and policies related to reliability, neutrality, and verifiability, defining and explaining each construct as it is understood within the Wikipedia community, and providing examples of how the policy is enacted and effectively battles misinformation, we illustrate the components and functions of the ethical assemblage. Following the review of these constructs, which we acknowledge as agentive in the construction of the encyclopedia's reliability, we introduce additional human and non/human agents that work in concert. By attending to the agencies of editors, administrators, bots, and readers, and in conjunctions with relevant information policies, we demonstrate how the construction of reliability is a distributed social and technical process resulting in ethical assemblages.

While our overall stance celebrates the ways in which the encyclopedia constructs reliability through these ethical assemblages, we acknowledge that Wikipedia is not a perfect system. The encyclopedia's second decade has been marked by broader realizations about its failure to fully represent diverse voices and global cultures in the curation of knowledge. In fact, Wikipedia's ambition to "collect the sum of all human knowledge"[18] is not a fully realized project. The encyclopedia suffers from massive gaps in representation and has had problems recruiting editors beyond its white, male, and Western base. These critiques are introduced in a discussion on Wikipedia's epistemological constraints and treated further in subsequent chapters of this book. Ultimately, we argue that it is the encyclopedia's evolving dynamism that lends potential to the project for critical media literacy, urging educators to attend to both the formal policies relating to reliability in Wikipedia, as well as the conditions and processes that are unspoken or opaque.

Through this exploration, this chapter also reconsiders previous prejudices regarding Wikipedia, many of which originated in academic circles. Our review of NPOV, Verifiability, and the distribution of information vetting provides an introductory lesson to Wikipedia readers, to help them move from the positionality of passive readers to more engaged readers, or even editors. While we acknowledge that Wikipedia's epistemological processes are not perfect, and there has been much discussion of systemic biases (see Chapters 3 and 4 for more on this), we argue for a broader recognition of Wikipedia's reliability as a process of critical media literacy that needs to be more widely adopted within and beyond formal academic institutions. We begin this exploration of relevant policies with a discussion of reliability, by attending to the guideline of "Reliability of source" (WP: RELIABLE), as it is understood in the community.

Reliability

Wikipedia is famous for being unreliable – except, this is not the case. Hundreds of comparative studies and other assessments have now vouched for the encyclopedia's reliability. Many of these studies are summarized within the English Wikipedia's guideline article on "Reliability of Wikipedia,"[19] which, among other things also identifies specific criteria for evaluating reliability in Wikipedia, for example:[20]

- Accuracy of information provided within articles
- Appropriateness of the images provided with the article
- Appropriateness of the style and focus of the article
- Susceptibility to, and exclusion and removal of, false information

- Comprehensiveness, scope, and coverage within articles and in the range of articles
- Identification of reputable third-party sources as citations
- Verifiability of statements by respected sources
- Stability of the articles
- Susceptibility to editorial and systemic bias
- Quality of writing

One of the earliest studies, first published in Nature in 2005, ascertained that Wikipedia was nearly as accurate as its (former) print contender *Encyclopaedia Britannica*. In this research, relevant experts conducted a blind review of comparative articles between the two encyclopedias, and found that "the difference in accuracy was not particularly great: the average science entry in Wikipedia contained around four inaccuracies; Britannica, about three."[21] Since then, numerous studies on subjects as diverse as medicine, crisis response, and as recent as the COVID-19 pandemic, have further solidified Wikipedia's currency and accuracy. In one study related to medicine and pharmacology, researchers "systematically analyzed the accuracy and completeness of drug information in the German and English language versions of Wikipedia in comparison to standard textbooks of pharmacology."[22] According to this research, the accuracy of pharmacological content in English and German language Wikipedias "was in the range between 99.6% and 100%...with an overall mean score of 99.7% +/− 0.17%."[23] Textbooks, on the other hand, were found to be only "55% +/− 12% for the German sources, and 74% +/− 14% for English textbooks."[24] Indeed, as early as 2007, Wikipedia was acknowledged as a reliable and rapid-response resource for information related to crisis events, particularly in the case of the Virginia Tech Massacre. Over 750,000 readers visited the article on the shooting within the first two days, and the Roanoke Times, a newspaper serving Blacksburg, acknowledged Wikipedia as a significant resource for understanding the event in its immediate aftermath.[25] Media coverage of the Wikipedia community's responsiveness speaks to the its overall reliability in terms of (chronological) currency; it also demonstrates the particular abilities and skills of editors to summarize reliable and verifiable secondary sources, which, as we will explain, are also significant aspects of the encyclopedia's reliability.

In 2017, the Poynter Institute, an organization devoted to ethical journalism and fact-checking, published an interview with Katherine Maher, executive director of the Wikimedia Foundation, in which Rebecca Iannucci asked, "What can fact-checkers learn from Wikipedia?" The resulting article identified three features of the Wikipedia community that aid in its immunity from problematic information: transparency, trust, and engagement.[26] As an organization dedicated to principles for ethical journalism and committed to working on global issues related to misinformation, it is especially notable that the Poynter institute turned to Wikipedia for understanding problematic information.

Furthermore, the three "protective" features identified in the Poynter interview became especially important in 2020 as Wikipedia continued to serve as a vital resource for fact-checking and battling problematic information on the web. In fact, Wikipedia was an important repository of reliable and accurate information during the COVID-19 Coronavirus pandemic. As acknowledged by the Wikimedia Foundation, "Since the start of COVID-19, a dedicated global network of volunteers has been creating, updating, and translating Wikipedia articles with vital information about the pandemic. These articles have been viewed more than 532 million times by people around the world."[27] Wikipedia's role in providing reliable public health information was also recognized fairly early in the pandemic by a number of news sources across the web. A few notable titles in March 2020 alone include Noam Cohen's *Wired* article "How Wikipedia Prevents the Spread of Coronavirus Misinformation,"[28] *Forbes'* "Like Zika, The Public Is Heading To Wikipedia During The COVID-19 Coronavirus Pandemic,"[29] and "Meet the Wikipedia editors fighting to keep coronavirus pages accurate" showed up on the *Daily Dot*.[30] In an age of misinformation, mass media had turned to praising Wikipedia for its accuracy.

Positive media regarding the encyclopedia's reliability and accuracy in 2020 begs the question: How did the encyclopedia go from something compared to a dietician prescribing fast food by a notable (if misguided) public intellectual, to one of the most respected global knowledge resources?

To answer this question, we look more deeply into its definition and enactment of reliability. Reliability, in Wikipedia, refers specifically to reliable sourcing, and the treatment of those sources in balance with others. The guideline for "Reliable sources" notes that "Wikipedia articles should be based on **reliable, published sources**, making sure that **all majority and significant minority views** that have appeared in those sources are covered (see Wikipedia:Neutral point of view)," and, as is typical with Wikipedia, they summarize this succinctly: "If no reliable sources can be found on a topic, Wikipedia should not have an article on it."[31] As is obvious from this policy statement, Wikipedia's policies for reliable sources intersect most with a number of other policies discussed in this chapter, especially NPOV, Verifiability, and Notability. Wikipedia depends on quality secondary sources to create tertiary article content, and the policy of Verifiability (the ability to verify a secondary source's content) also governs reliability. Such policies are the basis for the construction of reliability in Wikipedia, but they do not act alone. Rather, they are in constant assemblage with algorithms, editors, readers, and other agents in the ongoing creation of what we term *ethical assemblages*. In the following sections, we discuss how additional policies related to neutrality and verifiability also inform Wikipedia's reliability.

Neutrality

One of the oldest policies in Wikipedia (appearing in 2001), Neutral point of view (WP:NPOV) attempts to provide balanced coverage of actual sources, and, in doing so, potentially combats against amplification and opinion biases. In fact, both "No original research" and "Verifiability" policies have their origins in NPOV. NPOV is incredibly important to our discussion here, but also complex, as it ensures a lack of opinion-based writing, enforces neutral language and tone, as well as seeks to represent knowledge in a balanced manner according to reputable sources.

When secondary sources conflict, editors are encouraged to balance coverage by following NPOV, which builds credibility and aids editors in validating and verifying information accuracy and controlling bias. According to "Neutral point of view," all "encyclopedic content on Wikipedia must be written from a neutral point of view (NPOV), which means representing fairly, proportionately, and, as far as possible, without editorial bias, all of the significant views that have been published by reliable sources on a topic."[32] Furthermore, NPOV asserts that articles should explain opposing viewpoints rather than favoring one or the other, and that such favoring can happen in both the structure and content of an article. NPOV forwards an epistemology in which editors are requested to "describe disputes" rather than "engage" them. Finally, editors are expected to provide complete information from multiple reliable sources in order to best represent controversial subjects. The policy article on NPOV offers the following "principles" to help "achieve the level of neutrality that is appropriate for the encyclopedia":

- Avoid stating opinions as facts.
- Avoid stating seriously contested assertions as facts.

- Avoid stating facts as opinions.
- Prefer nonjudgmental language.
- Indicate the relative prominence of opposing views.[33]

NPOV goes beyond content to also suggest how an article's structure might be carefully safeguarded against biases: "Pay attention to headers, footnotes, or other formatting elements that might unduly favor one point of view, and watch out for structural or stylistic aspects that make it difficult for a reader to fairly and equally assess the credibility of all relevant and related viewpoints."[34] NPOV also requires equal weight for citing ideas, meaning that although the article should represent different aspects of the topic, only insofar as it is weighting these sides in a neutral manner. The part of the NPOV policy that deals with "Due" or "Undue" weighting is treads carefully concerning how to weigh articles appropriately, warning that "Wikipedia policy does not state or imply that every minority view or extraordinary claim needs to be presented along with commonly accepted mainstream scholarship as if they were of equal validity." This policy helps to combat the "all sides are valid" claim that plagues many fringe political arguments with spurious claims and beliefs. It also helps to properly weigh articles such as "Climate change" to accurately represent mainstream scholarship's overwhelming consensus on the matter, while giving extremely little space for competing claims, as the scholarship for competing claims are few and far between.

NPOV can be applied by editors in numerous ways, such as pointing out problems on a talk page or the offending editor's user page, annotating the offending page with a "[POV]" tag, filing a request for comment, or filing a report on the NPOV Noticeboard. However, because neutrality is not something as cut and dry as verifiability, editors rely on ongoing discussion and consensus-based decision-making. One of these methods of discussion is the NPOV Noticeboard, which is used as a way to bring other editors in to discuss neutrality of an article, hoping to find a balance in both language and representation. Editors are encouraged to discuss their disputes over the neutrality of an article rather than simply reverting content, as well as document disputes over controversial subjects. Instead of taking sides in the argument, editors are encouraged to document the different sides (balanced with sources, of course). Such discussions are accessible to anyone who visits the NPOV Noticeboard (given, of course, that one knows about such a thing).[35] Ultimately, NPOV helps to bring discussion around facts and representation which helps ensure that information remains and continues to remain accurate and representative of what is available to summarize. In the interpretation of NPOV policy toward the construction of reliability, Wikipedia encourages and facilitates critical discussion of information neutrality, which can help to balance out issues that arise in much of the rest of the Internet where "all sides" of an argument (even fringe ones) could be given equal space.

One recent example is a discussion of neutrality and undue weight on the (now merged) article "Reparative Therapy of Male Homosexuality," the title of a book and (discredited) pseudoscientific sexual orientation therapy created by Joseph Nicolosi. The central dispute involving NPOV related to this article was the use of multiple fringe sources that critiqued Amazon.com's decision to discontinue sales of the book. By attempting to use sources lambasting Amazon's decision for the establishment of the book itself as notable for inclusion in Wikipedia, the editor user:Freeknowlegecreator essentially gave undue weight to the subject of the book's removal.[36] NPOV describes undue weight (WP:UNDUE) by warning that "articles should not give minority views or aspects as much of or as detailed a description as more widely held views or widely supported aspects."[37] While multiple sources covered Amazon's action to remove the product from their website, these sources have limited relevance to the subject of the book itself. The issue was ultimately resolved when user: GPinkerton suggested merging the book's article with the article on the author (Nicolosi), and in doing so, also removed content related to the book's availability on Amazon. Also acknowledged through this discussion was the fact that user:Freeknowledgecreator was a sockpuppet[38] for user:Skoojal. Both accounts are now banned from the English Wikipedia.

While the case of "Reparative Therapy of Male Homosexuality" helps us understand particular elements of NPOV, and especially the policy of undue weight, it also demonstrates how these policies intervene in broader ideological battles being fought on and off the encyclopedia. User:Freeknowledgecreator was able to mount a campaign regarding the removal of Nicolosi's *Reparative Therapy of Male Homosexuality* from Amazon.com because there were plenty of (technically) verifiable sources to work with. The focus of these sources on the book's removal, however, was clearly in violation of undue weight. Demonstrating notability through secondary coverage of a book (as article topic) is not in itself problematic. In fact, a common strategy for ensuring notability of a new article is to compile numerous sources showing verifiable, secondary coverage. However, the secondary sources used, because they were mainly opinion pieces, and because they all had to do with one particular issue – the removal of the book from Amazon – were both unreliable and violated undue weight. That is, the scope and focus of the sources, because they only dealt with the very limited issue related to the book's removal, did not demonstrate broad, accurate, or reliable coverage.

Reading through the history of interactions between user:Freeknowledgecreator, their abuse of verifiability and undue weight, and the resulting editorial actions provides a glimpse into the often overt culture wars being waged on Wikipedia. By calling attention to the banning of the book, user:Freeknowledgecreator was clearly trying to defend Nicolosi's homophobic and pseudoscientific therapeutic practice. But because their editorial methods violated Wikipedia's information policies, that content, itself a type of misinformation, was removed. Ultimately, this example helps us understand how NPOV can be interpreted in Wikipedia, as well as the types of misinformation it can protect against. Furthermore, this example also demonstrates how multiple policies, editorial actions, and other factors inform the construction of reliability in Wikipedia.

Verifiability

Information validation in Wikipedia is largely a process of its Verifiability policy and related procedures. In short, the policy of Verifiability requires that any content added to mainspace must be "verifiable" by anyone encountering the information, and therefore referenced from a secondary and reliable source. Among other things, this coincides with the encyclopedia's strict adherence to a "No original research" (WP:NOR) policy, ensuring not only that opinions are unwelcome for Wikipedia content, but also excluding personal experience. When an editor attempts to make an addition to the encyclopedia, even if that addition involves information that the editor is confident of through first-hand experience, the content must be verified and verifiable through a secondary source. Verifiability is ensured through the careful practice of citation and reference to published, secondary sources, and content added must be directly from the cited sources.

Wikipedia policy further explains that the "burden to demonstrate verifiability lies with the editor who adds or restores material, and is satisfied by providing an inline citation to a reliable source that directly supports the contribution."[39] Such an assignment of responsibility for the burden of verifiability demonstrates the community's authorship of "rules of behavior," specific procedural arguments meant to carefully and thoroughly vet the addition of new content. Wikipedia's policy on Verifiability not only lays out the need for verifiable information taken from other published sources, but also clarifies what counts as a reliable source. This policy specifically states that "articles must be based on reliable, independent, published sources with a reputation for fact-checking and accuracy,"[40] particularly naming well-known journalistic and academic sources as the most ideal sources for verifiability. Numerous pages link from this policy page, with dozens of pages of text listing instances of reliable and unreliable sources, advice on how to think about information in context, and guidelines on how to make better decisions on sources. Despite being a seemingly simple statement about needing to verify information with an external source, the policy of Verifiability includes incredibly robust guidelines on the trustworthiness of information and how to make decisions about it. While demonstrating how verifiability works to construct reliability in Wikipedia, we also explore how the policy and its related practices connect with educational potential for increasing information literacy. Such educational opportunities, as we discuss in the preface, might be applied to anyone new to Wikipedia and unfamiliar with the policies and practices that shape its construction of reliability.

The policy of Verifiability is applied by editors on Wikipedia in numerous ways, as editors may challenge and revert unsourced content, annotate such content with a "[citation needed]" tag, or take editorial action to provide a verifiable reference for unsourced or poorly sourced content. All three constitute an immersive experience in information literacy, especially for new or novice Wikipedia users. Reversions of content, while not often easy to deal with as a new user, may be accompanied by an explanation about how the content violates a certain policy (e.g., Verifiability), providing an important lesson in how Wikipedia strives toward reliability. Furthermore, readers of Wikipedia encountering the "[citation needed]" tag are also exposed to the critical information literacy practices as they question the accuracy of the information provided and are introduced to Wikipedia policy. If the reader chooses to click on the tag, for example, they are directed to the information page on "[citation needed]" which also references and links to the policy page of Verifiability. The educational aspects of verifiability are further extended through Wikipedia subcultures and tools. For instance, WikiProject Reliability[41] identifies the project's primary goal as "ensur[ing] that content in articles is verifiable."[42] The WikiProject asks its members to "identify and tag claims that require verification with appropriate templates," "perform fact and reference checks for articles with verification templates," and "provide assistance with factual verification to editors."[43] A final example of the policy's application, as well as an educational feature, is the

Citation Hunt Tool, also linked to from WikiProject Reliability. This tool aggregates samples of mainspace article content that has been tagged in need of a citation and provides readers and would-be editors with "snippets" so that they might add a verifiable reference.[44] A leaderboard collects data on the editors who "fix" the most passages,[45] providing a gamified experience in information literacy intervention. These tasks engage members of the community in information literacy practices that work to ensure reliability and combat disinformation in the encyclopedia.

The "Citation needed" tag has become so common in Wikipedia that it has also entered into public discourse, to an extent, becoming demonstrative of the ways that Wikipedia has shaped society's understanding of reliability. Used to identify claims or facts that lack verifiable support from a reliable source, the tag is applied as a "request for another editor to verify a statement: a form of communication between members of a collaborative editing community. It is never, in itself, an "improvement" of an article."[46] First introduced in 2006 to encourage fact-checking and the use of verifiable sources, the tag has been used to identify at least 414,006 articles with unsourced statements.[47] Beyond Wikipedia, the annotation has become something of a popular meme, "used in real life to poke fun at public / corporate advertising [as well as political messaging] with dubious messages."[48] One of the most popular uses or remixes of the tag is a comic created by artist Randall Munroe, also known as xkcd. Self-published on xkcd.com, "a webcomic of romance, sarcasm, math, and language,"[49] the comic depicts a stick-figure (American) politician speaking at a podium to a crowd of additional stick-figures. Most notably, one individual in the crowd holds up a protest-style sign with the annotation "[citation needed]" as if to suggest to the politician that they may need to provide or check their source.

While this particular comic (entitled "Wikipedia Protestor"), and other memes related to the [citation needed] tag are certainly meant to invoke humor, they also serve as an example of the way Wikipedia practices related to reliability have entered into public (and popular) culture. Significantly, the comic by xkcd does not critique Wikipedia's reliability (the common public response, especially in 2007). Rather, it demonstrates how Wikipedia's practices and policies can shape and inform critical behaviors outside of the encyclopedia.

Beyond formal policy, the Wikimedia community also informs the construction of reliability in Wikipedia. Most recently, a group of Wikimedians has founded WikiCred, which "supports research, software projects, and Wikimedia events that explore information reliability and credibility." Formed in 2019 at WikiConference North America (which was also themed around information literacy), Wiki-Cred "also plans and supports small-production, high-scale initiatives in North America that focus on improving information literacy and credibility on the internet and beyond."[50] The program has already funded a number of grant projects related to information literacy and credibility in online platforms. *Sourcerer,* an anti-disinformation platform, for example, "leverages Wikipedia's credibility data to improve media literacy and combat disinformation on the web." More specifically, this program "provides a browser extension that informs Internet users of the quality of content they consume, and an API that enables developers to incorporate the Wikipedia community's reliability evaluations into new technologies."[51] This and other initiatives sponsored by WikiCred (who are in turn funded by Microsoft, Facebook, and Craig Newmark Philosophies) demonstrate how Wikipedia policies and practices are also beginning to shape a new landscape for online source evaluation and reliability.

Our exploration of policies related to Reliability, Neutrality, and Verifiability (as well as the implications, practices, and organizations related to these) demonstrates the robust and complex landscape through which Wikipedia constructs reliability. These policies make up a central element in how ethical assemblages operate in the encyclopedia. Such assemblages refer to the enacted and experiential programs assembled by multiple social actors, policies, and algorithmic processes through which the construction of reliability occurs. In the next section, we discuss the other major elements of these assemblages as they emerge and enact policy toward a distributed (or networked) information vetting process.

Distributed Information Vetting

Understanding Neutrality and Verifiability helps to illuminate how these Wikipedia policies function in the construction of reliability in the encyclopedia. In this section, we discuss how information vetting occurs as these policies become agentive alongside other human and non-human actors, such as editors, administrators, bots, readers.

Source evaluation especially, as it works toward the construction of reliability in Wikipedia, is distributed. Yochai Benkler, in an influential essay entitled "*Coase's Penguin, or, Linux and* the Nature of the Firm," first defined Wikipedia's unique economic model as commons-based peer production (or CBPP). Benkler used the term CBPP to "distinguish it from the property- and contract-based modes of firms and markets" and identified CBPP's central characteristic as allowing "groups of individuals [to] successfully collaborate on large-scale projects following a diverse cluster of motivational drives and social signals, rather than either market prices or managerial commands."[52] Such collaboration, Benkler continues, "depends on very large aggregations of individuals independently scouring their information environment in search of opportunities to be creative in small or large increments."[53] Like CBPP, the distributed construction of reliability on Wikipedia depends on social collaboration. However, we must also make considerations beyond the social to include non-human agents as part of these ethical assemblages. Systems and algorithms associated with automated confirmation (autoconfirmation) and the use of automated bots also act in concert within this assemblage to promote reliability and ward off misinformation on Wikipedia.[54]

Autoconfirmation and confirmation of editors, as processes which provide enhanced privileges to user accounts (as discussed in Chapter 1), provide a stark rebuttal to the historic concern over Wikipedia's crowdsourced model of "if anyone can edit then anything goes." Certainly, this was at the center of the concern that Michael Gorman shared when he debased Wikipedia's intellectual "nutrition." This concern is answered from a procedural point of view through user access levels because although "anyone can edit," not everyone has access to all the features on Wikipedia. New users on Wikipedia (those that have accounts less than four days old and with less than ten edits) are restricted in terms of the editorial actions they can take, as they are unable to "create articles, move pages, edit semi-protected pages, and upload files."[55] Once they meet or exceed the requirements, new users become "autoconfirmed" and are then able to perform these functions.

An additional early line of protection against misinformation which helps work toward reliability in Wikipedia is the use of automated bots. Wikipedia defines a bot as an "automated tool that carries out repetitive and mundane tasks to maintain the 47,329,838 pages of the English Wikipedia." The English Wikipedia currently has 2,345 bot tasks approved, and over 900 bots listed, the most active bot having made over 4 million edits.[56] Because bots have the capability to make rapid changes to the encyclopedia, their programming and activity is closely monitored and governed by a community-devised "bot policy," which lays out expectations that bots "meet high standards before they are approved for use on designated tasks."[57] Among other functions, bots patrol editors' contributions and alert administrators of potential vandalism and other types of problematic information.[58] In general,

Wikipedia, as a volunteer-run community site, relies on heavy policing by bots so as to streamline repetitive tasks and reduce headaches for editors and administrators.

Wikipedia's use of user access levels and bots demonstrates how the community has devised policies and socially deliberated rules to prevent problematic information and increase the site's overall credibility. While bots and user access levels provide an automated (and often behind-the-scenes) safeguard against problematic information, policies such as Verifiability and No original research ensure that the sources used to build articles are accessible, reliable, and verifiable. Additionally, the policy of Neutral Point of View further contributes to the ethical assemblages found in Wikipedia by challenging editors to add content that demonstrates balanced coverage of sources, represents significant perspectives, avoiding bias, and providing due weight.

Understanding and acknowledging (and maybe even a bit of celebrating) the methods through which Wikipedia constructs reliability helps to open up a space for better questions and critical engagement. However, Wikipedia is not a perfect system. In broad terms, Wikipedia's goal to "collect the sum of all human knowledge"[59] is not a fully realized project as massive gaps in representation limit the encyclopedia's coverage while the community has failed to adequately recruit editors beyond its white, male, and Western base. These problems are part of a discussion on Wikipedia's epistemological constraints, yet they also represent particular failings in terms of Wikipedia's reliability to fully represent global human knowledge.

Print Culture as Exclusionary Epistemology

Wikipedia's project to gather the sum of all human knowledge is an incredibly ambitious one, if only for its insistence that the endeavor itself is even possible given the constraints of the encyclopedia itself. For example, the encyclopedia's policy for Verifiability, while a key element in the construction of reliability, also significantly limits its capacity for truly representing global knowledge. Not all knowledge exists in written, published form, yet the encyclopedia continues to adhere to print culture to verify factual claims. Such a paradox has been noted by Peter Gallert and Maja van der Velden:

> Wikipedia as an encyclopedia is rooted in a culture of writing—not simply in the usage of a writing system to express and conserve thoughts, but in the almost exclusive usage of written sources for the body of its content. In its endeavor to systemize and codify

> the knowledge of mankind it voluntarily restricts itself to facts that are supported by reliable, published, third-party sources, as defined by its editor community.[60]

Wikipedia's adherence to print culture has allowed the community to develop effective policies for reliability, but also prevents it from accomplishing its encyclopedic goal of becoming a global human knowledge source. More specifically, the emphasis on verifiable print sources plays a significant role in the marginalization of indigenous knowledge cultures, especially when their knowledge is stored and transmitted orally. Peter Gallert and Maja van der Velden further explain this process of marginalization.

> For many aspects of the culture, tradition, and knowledge of indigenous people, there exist no or insufficient written records. This puts indigenous knowledge in Wikipedia, particularly on its largest language edition, the English Wikipedia, into a disadvantageous situation. Oral information transmission is not regarded as a way of publishing by the online encyclopedia, knowledge keepers are often believed to be too close to their narrative's subjects to follow a neutral point of view, and passing on songs and stories is not seen as a reliable way of preserving knowledge.[61]

Unfortunately, this failure to engage oral knowledge practices represents only one of many issues relating to unreliable coverage in Wikipedia. Researchers, academics, and Wikimedians alike have also addressed problems related to the encyclopedia's gender gap, the condition in which the overwhelming majority of editors in the encyclopedia are male, and the resulting lack of coverage of certain topics because of this homogeneous demographic, as discussed in Chapter 3.[62] A lack of coverage not only means missing articles on notable topics or figures, but also articles that are often under-developed. In both cases, the reliability of Wikipedia suffers due to a lack of coverage of marginalized topics.

Given the systemic issues related to indigenous knowledge and gender discussed above, is Wikipedia's ambition to reflect a global constituency even possible? Toward the end of his brief essay "What is an Encyclopedia? An Historical Overview from Pliny to Wikipedia," Dan O'Sullivan explains why the project's ambition will always fail, writing:

> The illusion of a totalizing drive for universal knowledge – a project that is manifestly impossible to achieve, even with the most advanced technology and the enthusiastic cooperation of

> thousands – is also quite inappropriate in the emergent postmodern, skeptical, and multicultural world of today. Indeed, knowledge cannot be exhaustively collected and stored in this manner but is always tied to the local time and situation in which it was developed and deployed, constantly in a state of flux.[63]

O'Sullivan's critique is apt. In many ways, Wikipedia's ambition for universal knowledge (itself an ambition of the encyclopedic genre more broadly) is an impossible goal.[64] At the same time, that goal has inspired countless volunteers to contribute. Despite its failures, Wikipedia remains the most comprehensive and equitable encyclopedia ever created. Much of that success, furthermore, is due to its ability to respond to knowledge curation as an ongoing and never-ending process. O'Sullivan recognizes that knowledge is "constantly in a state of flux" – so too does the Wikipedia community. This recognition, in part, is due to the community's understanding of the affordances of wiki technology as a platform for constructing the encyclopedia.

Wikipedia as Epistemology in Process

Because of its innovative application of the wiki platform for large-scale peer production, Wikipedia represents an epistemology in process: one that is always evolving alongside social, cultural, and technological influences. Indeed, the encyclopedia's fifth pillar states that "Wikipedia has no firm rules." Instead of rules, Wikipedia has "policies and guidelines" whose "content and interpretation can evolve over time."[65] Just as policies for verifiability and neutral point of view evolve and emerge through social processes, other policies may also be developed. Furthermore, it is this unfinished and in-process state that helps to reconcile the encyclopedia's failures. To forgive its failures, we must see Wikipedia as always in-flux. And we must also realize that it can change. This change begins with a new attention – not just to the development and diversification of mainspace articles, but to the meta-space in which Wikipedians develop, negotiate, and share relevant information policies. It is this project namespace that helps us discover the underground discourses governing the representation of reality. Furthermore, it is the flux and negotiation that occurs in these spaces, ultimately, that demonstrates the encyclopedia's capability to value both the impossible ambitions of the encyclopedic genre *and* the complicated postmodern reality of knowledge as highly contextual and in-flux.[66] In the final section, we call on our readers to shift their focus from Wikipedia's problems, and instead, attend to its development of policies related to reliability in order to provide opportunities understanding reliability in digital ecologies.

Implications for Public Knowledge

In providing a review and analysis of formal and informal policies and procedures in this chapter, we have also offered an accessible entry point to begin understanding Wikipedia's construction of reliability from a more nuanced perspective. As Wikipedia continues to mature,[67] there is an even more urgent need to sweep away the many negative narratives that plagued its early years. Policies such as NPOV and Verifiability serve as especially important first-impression constructs in Wikipedia because these policies demonstrate to the uninitiated or novice Wikipedia reader two things. First, Wikipedia is a community that deliberates on and is guided by very specific information policies (that operate on both formal, "visible" levels as well as through functions that are more "hidden"). And second, that those policies are extremely effective as they shape information accuracy and reliability in the encyclopedia.

The significance of Wikipedia's information processes cannot be overstated. Wikipedia constructs its representation of reality in part through its construction of reliability. In essence, the encyclopedia decides "what counts" as knowledge as it evaluates, processes, and consequently validates information. As we acknowledge these formal policies, we also keep in mind the unspoken work of underlying epistemologies (especially those that value print sources over other types of sources), and remember that such epistemologies also shape how and what the encyclopedia deems knowledge. In many ways, reliability in Wikipedia is a double-edged sword, as it is accompanied by both advantages and disadvantages. Verifiability, for example, helps to validate information and promote accuracy and trust in the encyclopedia. At the same time, the focus on print or written secondary sources, to the exclusion of other types of knowledge, limits Wikipedia's ability to fully become reliable in terms of coverage of marginalized topics, or topics which have been developed through knowledge-making practices beyond print. These lessons are important for the general public that consumes and uses the encyclopedia, as well as for anyone that identifies as a newcomer to Wikipedia.

Understanding even a small piece of how information becomes knowledge in Wikipedia can increase information literacy skills across other digital platforms, especially in terms of becoming more active and critical evaluators of digital information. More specifically, participation in Wikipedia's information vetting policies and procedures provides opportunities for critical source evaluation and thinking through distributed information literacy processes. While previous research has found that formal Wikipedia-based education provides opportunities for effective teaching and learning about the reliability of sources,[68] we see Wikipedia as instructive in theorizing and teaching reliability itself, for all kinds of users beyond academia, especially as it relates to digital information ecologies.

Moving forward from information to the construction of knowledge, in Chapter 3 we turn to another significant policy in Wikipedia, and one that is again, widely misunderstood: notability – and how it further impacts what is included. These two elements make up the major components in how policies and guidelines on Wikipedia manage and limit the inclusion of information and topics get included – on what articles get included and what gets included in them. This sets the stage for understanding the major systems which Wikipedia utilizes to formulate its representation of reality.

Notes

1 As discussed in Chapter 1, unless otherwise noted, the majority of our discussions refer to the English language version of Wikipedia in this book.
2 "Wikipedia: Size of Wikipedia," Wikipedia, last modified September 20, 2020, https://en.wikipedia.org/w/index.php?title=Wikipedia:Size_of_Wikipedia&oldid=979316349.
3 Michael Gorman, "Jabberwiki: The Educational Response, Part II," Encyclopedia Britannica Blog, accessed December 1, 2020, http://blogs.Δbritannica.com/2007/06/jabberwiki-the-educational-response-part-ii/.
4 Ibid.
5 Wikipedia: Neutral Point of View," Wikipedia, last modified November 10, 2001, https://en.wikipedia.org/w/index.php?title=Wikipedia:Neutral_point_of_view&oldid=334854039.
6 "Wikipedia:Verifiability," Wikipedia, last modified August 2, 2003, https://en.wikipedia.org/w/index.php?title=Wikipedia:Verifiability&oldid=1230640.
7 Stephen Harrison, "Happy 18th Birthday, Wikipedia. Let's Celebrate the Internet's Good Grown-Up," *Washington Post*, January 14, 2019, https://www.washingtonpost.com/opinions/happy-18th-birthday-wikipedia-lets-celebrate-the-internets-good-grown-up/2019/01/14/e4d854cc-1837-11e9-9ebf-c5fed1b7a081_story.html.; Peter Forsyth, "How Wikipedia Dodged Public Outcry Plaguing Social Media Platforms," Wikistrategies.net, August 23, 2018, https://wikistrategies.net/how-wikipedia-dodged-public-outcry-plaguing-social-media-platforms/.; R. Cooke, "Wikipedia Is the Last Best Place on the Internet," Wired, 2020, https://www.wired.com/story/wikipedia-online-encyclopedia-best-place-internet/.

8 Adam R. Brown, "Wikipedia as a Data Source for Political Scientists: Accuracy and Completeness of Coverage," *PS: Political Science and Politics* 44, no. 2 (2011): 339–343. https://www.jstor.org/stable/41319920; Jim Giles, "Internet Encyclopaedias Go Head to Head," *Nature* 438, no. 7070 (December 1, 2005): 900–901. https://doi.org/10.1038/438900a; Thomas J. Hwang, Florence T. Bourgeois, and John D. Seeger, "Drug Safety in the Digital Age," *The New England Journal of Medicine* 370, no. 26 (June 26, 2014): 2460–2462. https://doi.org/10.1056/NEJMp1401767; Jona Kräenbring, Tika Monzon Penza, Joanna Gutmann et al., "Accuracy and Completeness of Drug Information in Wikipedia: A Comparison with Standard Textbooks of Pharmacology," *PLOS ONE* 9, no. 9 (September 24, 2014). https://doi.org/10.1371/journal.pone.0106930; Dario Taraborelli, "Seven Years after Nature, Pilot Study Compares Wikipedia Favorably to Other Encyclopedias in Three Languages," *Diff* (blog), August 2, 2012, https://diff.wikimedia.org/2012/08/02/seven-years-after-nature-pilot-study-compares-wikipedia-favorably-to-other-encyclopedias-in-three-languages/.

9 Carolyn Jack, "Lexicon of Lies: Terms for Problematic Information," *Data & Society* 3 (2017), https://datasociety.net/wp-content/uploads/2017/08/DataAndSociety_LexiconofLies.pdf.

10 Ibid., 2–3.

11 Ibid., 1.

12 Garth Jowett and Victoria O'Donnell, *Propaganda & Persuasion*, 7th ed. (Los Angeles: SAGE, 2019).

13 Omer Benjakob, "Why Wikipedia Is Immune to Coronavirus," Haaretz.com, accessed December 4, 2020, https://www.haaretz.com/us-news/.premium.MAGAZINE-why-wikipedia-is-immune-to-coronavirus-1.8751147.

14 Wikimedia Foundation, "Wikipedia and COVID-19," April 13, 2020, https://wikimediafoundation.org/covid19/data/.

15 Scot Barnett and Casey Andrew Boyle, eds., *Rhetoric, through Everyday Things*, Rhetoric, Culture, and Social Critique (Tuscaloosa: The University of Alabama Press, 2016); Laurie E. Gries, *Still Life with Rhetoric: A New Materialist Approach for Visual Rhetorics* (Logan: Utah State University Press, 2015); Paul Walker, "A Rhythmic Refrain: Britain's Mass-Observation as Rhetorical Assemblage," *Rhetoric Review* 35, no. 3 (July 2, 2016): 212–225. https://doi.org/10.1080/07350198.2016.1178690.

16 Gilles Deleuze and Claire Parnet, *Dialogues* (New York: Columbia University Press, 1987), 69.

17 It is important to note that our theorization of reliability as an outcome of ethical assemblages is not one that is necessarily shared by the Wikipedia community.

18 Roblimo, "Wikipedia Founder Jimmy Wales Responds," *Slashdot* (blog), July 28, 2004, https://slashdot.org/story/04/07/28/1351230/wikipedia-founder-jimmy-wales-responds.

19 "Reliability of Wikipedia," Wikipedia, last modified July 17, 2020, https://en.wikipedia.org/w/index.php?title=Reliability_of_Wikipedia&oldid=968078346.

20 "Reliability of Wikipedia."

21 Jim Giles, "Internet Encyclopaedias Go Head to Head," *Nature* 438, no. 7070 (December 1, 2005): 900–901. https://doi.org/10.1038/438900a.

22 Kräenbring et al., "Accuracy and Completeness of Drug Information," 1.

23 Kräenbring et al., 5.
24 Ibid., 4.
25 Noam Cohen, "The Latest on Virginia Tech, From Wikipedia," *The New York Times*, April 23, 2007, Technology, https://www.nytimes.com/2007/04/23/technology/23link.html.
26 Rebecca Ianucci, "What Can Fact-Checkers Learn from Wikipedia? We Asked the Boss of Its Nonprofit Owner," *Poynter* (blog), July 6, 2017, https://www.poynter.org/fact-checking/2017/what-can-fact-checkers-learn-from-wikipedia-we-asked-the-boss-of-its-nonprofit-owner/.
27 "Wikipedia and COVID-19."
28 Noam Cohen, "How Wikipedia Prevents the Spread of Coronavirus Misinformation," Wired, accessed August 2, 2020, https://www.wired.com/story/how-wikipedia-prevents-spread-coronavirus-misinformation/.
29 Farah Qaiser, "Like Zika, The Public Is Heading To Wikipedia During The COVID-19 Coronavirus Pandemic," *Forbes*, accessed August 2, 2020,https://www.forbes.com/sites/farahqaiser/2020/03/18/like-zika-the-public-is-heading-to-wikipedia-during-the-covid-19-coronavirus-pandemic/.
30 Mikael Thalen, "Meet the Wikipedia Editors Fighting to Keep Coronavirus Pages Accurate," *The Daily Dot*, March 24, 2020, https://www.dailydot.com/debug/wikipedia-coronavirus-page/.
31 "Wikipedia: Reliable Sources," Wikipedia, last modified July 1, 2020, https://en.wikipedia.org/w/index.php?title=Wikipedia:Reliable_sources&oldid=965472450.
32 "Wikipedia: Neutral Point of View," Wikipedia, last modified July 12, 2020, https://en.wikipedia.org/w/index.php?title=Wikipedia:Neutral_point_of_view&oldid=967336587.
33 Ibid.
34 Ibid.
35 "Wikipedia: Neutral Point of View/Noticeboard," Wikipedia, last modified July 12, 2020, https://en.wikipedia.org/w/index.php?title=Wikipedia:Neutral_point_of_view/Noticeboard&oldid=967345749.
36 "Wikipedia: Neutral Point of View/Noticeboard#Reparative Therapy," Wikipedia, last modified July 12, 2020, https://en.wikipedia.org/w/index.php?title=Wikipedia:Neutral_point_of_view/Noticeboard&oldid=967345749.
37 "Wikipedia: Neutral Point of View," Wikipedia, last modified December 5, 2020, https://en.wikipedia.org/w/index.php?title=Wikipedia:Neutral_point_of_view&oldid=992523446.
38 In Wikipedia, a sockpuppet refers to an additional account held by a user in order to bypass formal rules or editing sanctions. See, "Wikipedia: Sockpuppetry," Wikipedia, last modified December 31, 2020, https://en.wikipedia.org/w/index.php?title=Wikipedia:Sockpuppetry&oldid=997525229.
39 "Wikipedia: Verifiability," Wikipedia, last modified November 29, 2020, https://en.wikipedia.org/w/index.php?title=Wikipedia:Verifiability&oldid=991232984.
40 Ibid.
41 In Wikipedia, WikiProjects are initiatives set up to improve a certain topic area or issue in the encyclopedia. Think of these groups as task forces, ranging in size, whose members identify and improve some aspect of Wikipedia.

42 "Wikipedia:WikiProject Reliability," Wikipedia, last modified November 24, 2020, https://en.wikipedia.org/w/index.php?title=Wikipedia:WikiProject_Reliability&oldid=990325388.
43 Ibid.
44 "Citation Hunt," accessed December 6, 2020, https://citationhunt.toolforge.org/en?id=1f50f263.
45 Ibid.
46 "Wikipedia: Citation Needed," Wikipedia, last modified July 7, 2020, https://en.wikipedia.org/w/index.php?title=Wikipedia:Citation_needed&oldid=966577082.
47 "Category: All Articles with Unsourced Statements," Wikipedia, last modified October 12, 2020, https://en.wikipedia.org/w/index.php?title=Category:All_articles_with_unsourced_statements&oldid=983216779.
48 Know Your Meme, "[Citation Needed]," last modified January 21, 2021, https://knowyourmeme.com/memes/citation-needed.
49 xkcd, "Wikipedian Protester," accessed January 21, 2021, https://xkcd.com/285/.
50 WikiCred, "WikiCred," accessed December 6, 2020, https://www.wikicred.org/.
51 Ibid.
52 Benkler, "Coase's Penguin," 3.
53 Ibid., p. 7.
54 Jialei Jiang and Matthew A. Vetter, "The Good, the Bot, and the Ugly: Problematic Information and Critical Media Literacy in the Postdigital Era," *Postdigital Science and Education* 2, no. 1 (2019): 78–94. https://doi.org/10.1007/s42438-019-00069-4.
55 "Wikipedia: User Access Levels," Wikipedia, last modified December 7, 2020, https://en.wikipedia.org/w/index.php?title=Wikipedia:User_access_levels&oldid=992855133.
56 "Wikipedia: Bots," Wikipedia, last modified December 7, 2020, https://en.wikipedia.org/w/index.php?title=Wikipedia:Bots&oldid=992898959; "Wikipedia: List of Bots by Number of Edits," Wikipedia, last modified March 3, 2020, https://en.wikipedia.org/w/index.php?title=Wikipedia:List_of_bots_by_number_of_edits&oldid=943632202.
57 "Wikipedia: Bot Policy," Wikipedia, last modified September 29, 2020, https://en.wikipedia.org/w/index.php?title=Wikipedia:Bot_policy&oldid=981013140.
58 R. Stuart Geiger, "The Lives of Bots," in *Critical Point of View: A Wikipedia Reader*, eds. Lovink Geert and Nathaniel Tkacz (Amsterdam: Institute of Network Cultures, 2011), 78–93.
59 Roblimo, "Wikipedia Founder Jimmy Wales Responds," *Slashdot* (blog), July 28, 2004, https://slashdot.org/story/04/07/28/1351230/wikipedia-founder-jimmy-wales-responds.
60 Peter Gallert and Maja Van der Velden, "Reliable Sources for Indigenous Knowledge: Dissecting Wikipedia's Catch-22," in *Embracing Indigenous Knowledge in a New Technology Design Paradigm*, eds. Nicola J. Bidwell and Heike Winschiers-Theophilus (Indigenous Knowledge Technology Conference, 2013). http://ir.nust.na/jspui/handle/10628/409.
61 Ibid.
62 Noam Cohen,"Define Gender Gap? Look Up Wikipedia's Contributor List," *The New York Times*, January 30, 2011. Business. https://www.

nytimes.com/2011/01/31/business/media/31link.html; Heather Ford and Judy Wajcman, "'Anyone Can Edit', Not Everyone Does: Wikipedia's Infrastructure and the Gender Gap," *Social Studies of Science* 47, no. 4 (August 1, 2017): 511–527, https://doi.org/10.1177/0306312717692172; Leigh Gruwell, "Wikipedia's Politics of Exclusion: Gender, Epistemology, and Feminist Rhetorical (In)Action," *Computers and Composition* 37 (September 1, 2015): 117–131, https://doi.org/10.1016/j.compcom.2015.06.009; Matthew A. Vetter, John Andelfinger, Shahla Asadolahi, Wenqi Cui, Jialei Jiang, Tyrone Jones, and Zeeshan F. Siddique, "Wikipedia's Gender Gap and Disciplinary Praxis: Representing Women Scholars in Digital Rhetoric and Writing Fields," *Journal of Multimodal Rhetorics* 2, no. 2 (2018); Adrianne Wadewitz, "Wikipedia's Gender Gap and the Complicated Reality of Systemic Gender Bias," *HASTAC* (blog), 2013. https://www.hastac.org/blogs/wadewitz/2013/07/26/wikipedias-gender-gap-and-complicated-reality-systemic-gender-bias; Claudia Wagner, David Garcia, and Markus Strohmaier, "It's a Man's Wikipedia? Assessing Gender Inequality in an Online Encyclopedia," (Palo Alto, CA: AAAI, 2015): 454–463, https://www.aaai.org/ocs/index.php/ICWSM/ICWSM15/paper/view/10585.

63 Dan O'Sullivan, "What Is an Encyclopedia? A Brief Overview from Pliny to Wikipedia," in *Critical Point of View: A Wikipedia Reader*, eds. Geert Lovink and Nathaniel Tkacz (Amsterdam: Institute of Network Cultures, 2011), 10. https://papers.ssrn.com/abstract=2075015.

64 Matthew A. Vetter, "Possible Enlightenments: Wikipedia's Encyclopedic Promise and Epistemological Failure," in *Wikipedia @ Twenty: Stories from an Incomplete Revolution*, eds. Joseph Reagle and Jackie Koerner (Cambridge, MA: MIT Press, 2020), 285–295.

65 "Wikipedia: Five Pillars," Wikipedia, last modified September 11, 2020, https://en.wikipedia.org/w/index.php?title=Wikipedia:Five_pillars&oldid=977945932.

66 For a more robust treatment of Wikipedia as a site for knowledge curation informed by both Enlightenment Era and postmodernist ideology, see: Matthew A. Vetter, "Possible Enlightenments: Wikipedia's Encyclopedic Promise and Epistemological Failure," in *Wikipedia @ Twenty: Stories from an Incomplete Revolution*, eds. Joseph Reagle and Jackie Koerner (Cambridge, MA: MIT Press, 2020), 285–295.

67 The encyclopedia celebrated its twentieth birthday in January of 2021.

68 Matthew A. Vetter, Zachary J. McDowell, and Mahala Stewart, "From Opportunities to Outcomes: The Wikipedia-Based Writing Assignment," *Computers and Composition* 52 (June 1, 2019): 53–64. https://doi.org/10.1016/j.compcom.2019.01.008.

3 What Counts as Knowledge

Notability, Knowledge Gaps, and Exclusionary Practices

> Whatever patterns are introduced will be continuously modified through the exceedingly variegated and subtle interchange of subjective meanings that goes on.
>
> —Peter L. Berger, *The Social Construction of Reality*

Introduction

On October 2, 2018, Donna Strickland became the third woman ever to be awarded the Nobel Prize in Physics. She was the first woman to achieve this distinction in 55 years, joining Maria Goeppert Mayer (1964), and Marie Curie (1903). Despite Strickland's accomplished scientific career leading up to this momentous occasion, until the day of the award, she did not have a page on Wikipedia, at least one that was published on mainspace. We say published because the initial page for Strickland was written more than four years prior, on March 7, 2014, only to be nominated for speedy deletion (and deleted) that very day. It took a Nobel prize for her page to be deemed "notable" enough for inclusion.

The lack of a Wikipedia page for a Nobel Laureate until the award was announced struck a nerve amongst many that have been concerned about the way Wikipedia decides what to include in the encyclopedia. Strickland was not the first, nor will she be the last, person excluded from the encyclopedia due to a guideline known as "Notability" (or WP:N). In its very basic sense, notability is a "test used by editors to determine whether a given topic warrants its own article."[1] The test seems rather straightforward as it is to understand whether the topic (or person) has "received significant coverage in reliable sources,"[2] but much like everything else on Wikipedia, it remains incredibly complicated in how it is employed.

Notability is one of the most important policies on Wikipedia as it serves as a checksum to protect Wikipedia from a variety of

DOI: 10.4324/9781003094081-3

unimportant topics (or misinformation). Ensuring that the topics have coverage in independent reliable sources means that the information has been vetted as, to quote *New York Times* owner Adolph S. Ochs, "news that's fit to print."[3] Building on reliability, covered extensively in Chapter 2, the policy of notability expects numerous *reliable* sources to ensure that not only is the information deemed worthy of inclusion, but that it is reflective of a collective focus by producers of secondary sources. Notability, in this sense, ensures that the topic at hand is not just a one-off, and that coverage must be sufficient to consider the coverage of a topic or person as "knowledge." However, relying on journalistic sources means that Wikipedia can only include information that has been deemed printworthy by editorial teams that potentially, both historically and currently, suffer from biases. These biases can result in exclusionary reporting to begin with, covering particular topics or people and ignoring others, which can then be amplified and compounded by Wikipedia's policies and editorial discretion when determining "notability," resulting in significantly limited coverage of important topics and people. These compounded biases result in a continuous filtration of knowledge through multiple systems, limiting what appears in Wikipedia by this compound system of filtration biases, excluding all but those that pass numerous, and often un-critiqued, gatekeepers.

Ironically for someone not deemed notable until receiving the highest award in the world for their field, Donna Strickland's story of exclusion on Wikipedia received *significant* press coverage, and numerous sources called out Wikipedia for its perceived exclusionary practices in regard to notability of Strickland and other female scientists. The Executive Director of the Wikimedia Foundation, Katherine Maher, responded to the controversy, acknowledging the issue along with pointing out the larger issues included, stating that "[Wikipedia is] a mirror of the world's biases, not the source of them."[4] Maher notes that since the Notability policy is based on the amount of press coverage a person has received, Wikipedia's policy, for better or worth, can (at best) only reflect the topic's printed coverage. Furthermore, since women in many professions have historically received less coverage than their male colleagues, Wikipedia inherits this representation issue due to the larger systemic biases. Of course, these biases are not limited to gender representation and extend to marginalized biographies, stories, histories, and places all over. In this manner, Notability acts as a double-edged sword, both as an exclusionary protection against "everything under the sun needs its own page" and also acting as gatekeeping that can significantly limit representation of already marginalized topics and voices.

Practices of inclusion and exclusion in Wikipedia are not limited to Notability, of course. All archival and encyclopedic projects, at their core, are exclusionary – that is, they cannot include and preserve everything in their collection. As Wikipedia hopes to collect "the sum of all human knowledge," the exclusions here are telling to how it functions, and how it preserves its own identity as an encyclopedia with such a lofty goal. Wikipedia's definition of what counts as "knowledge" here is especially interesting in the way it represents and shapes reality – reliability as a substitute for truth, and notability (in a sense, a collection of reliable "facts") as a substitute for determining what "knowledge" counts. This does not necessarily mean this is a bad thing, it just happens to be the way that Wikipedia and its community have decided is the best way to make sense of things. As discussed in Chapter 2, Wikipedia's policies are exclusionary for good reason – Wikipedia hopes to ensure its own reliability by evaluating and using (only) reliable sources. Reliability is the foundation on which Wikipedia continues to prosper, even as it remains veritably geriatric (for an Internet site) as it recently passed 20 years of age. Notability here is no different at its core – Wikipedia might hope to represent "the sum of all human knowledge"[5] but it also seeks to ensure that its sourcing remains reliable and the things represented are not a whimsical addition of someone's great uncle without any historical significance. Beyond notability of an article's topic, however, is also what gets included within the article (once it has been deemed notable, that is) – what information is pertinent and where should it exist are hotly debated topics within the Wikipedia community. Finally, when seeking to include "the sum of all human knowledge," it is also important to think about the accessibility of this knowledge that serves as Wikipedia's grist so that a) editors can glean knowledge from the best sources possible (despite some being behind paywalls), and b) readers have access to source material so that they can expand their own knowledge beyond that of an encyclopedia article.

The following pages of this chapter explore these important and exclusionary protocols, practices, and processes that determine what the Wikipedia community deems worthy of inclusion in the "sum of all human knowledge" and how what is (and is not) included shapes the largest repository of knowledge in the world. Through exploration of what Berger notes as the interchange "subjective meanings" that, in turn, must be examined as a pattern to help trace the larger concerns, we examine these notability guidelines, various policies and practices, cognitive and systemic biases, decision-making processes, article information inclusion, and accessibility of sources. Through all of this, this chapter will help to show how what constitutes Wikipedia's mainspace (and indeed the construction of the knowledge within Wikipedia's representation of "reality") remains a result of a complex assemblage of policies and the unspoken rules and limitations that govern their implementation by a dedicated, loving, and ultimately imperfect community.

Everything Cannot Be Everything: Defining through Exclusion

Instead of beginning at the Notability policy to establish how Wikipedia decides whether something is included, understanding Wikipedia's scope as one that is *predominantly exclusive* remains imperative to establishing an understanding of Wikipedia's processes. In particular (and more of this in Chapter 4), the ways in which the community functions *as* exclusionary both defines what Wikipedia *is* and also what it can become. This is not necessarily a negative thing – editors of Wikipedia must remain diligently exclusive in regard to information coming into Wikipedia. As with any "open" space on the Internet, a significant amount of garbage flows into it. Moderating inclusion on Wikipedia remains an inexhaustible task for Wikipedians, and the nonstop nature of this inevitably both allows some garbage through, as well as gate-keeps important work from surviving long enough to improve. Hopefully, eventually, the garbage gets spotted and "taken out," but once things are gone, they are often gone for good unless a diligent editor continues to struggle against confusing, complex, and frustrating editorial policies and decision-making. Stories abound in regard to frustrations related to deletionist[6] tendencies on Wikipedia, but often go unnoticed unless a spotlight (much like in the case of Donna Strickland) illuminates the situation.

In Spring of 2014, Bryce Peake, an Assistant Professor at UMBC, created a category on Wikipedia called "Schools Announced Under Investigation for Sexual Violence Policy Violations," which linked 72 colleges and universities "under investigation" for violations under Title IX and the Clery Act. In addition, Peake also made numerous additions to the pages, documenting issues from a variety of secondary sources. All told, Peake estimated he spent about 20 hours attempting to represent information about sexual assault issues on colleges and universities on Wikipedia, only to find his changes reverted within a day of finishing the project, with editors citing multiple policies (WP:UNDUE, WP:RELIABILITY, WP:RECENTISM, and WP:POV) to argue for reversion.[7]

Peake's engagement with Wikipedia is one that highlights what he refers to as "WP:THREATENING2MEN," and underscores a major concern about the limits of inclusion within Wikipedia, both from a topical perspective (individual pages and categories), as well as what can and should be included in individual pages.[8] Peake notes a major way that Wikipedians facilitate the exclusion of information is through what a University of Washington and HP Labs project refers to as "power plays," in which editors argue rhetorically for exclusion or deletion utilizing vague and ambiguous language in certain policies.[9] This is just one example of an unfortunate experience with attempting to include (arguably) relevant information on Wikipedia, which was met with confusing and concerning behavior by editors. Although Bryce's term highlights some of the (major) issues around exclusion on Wikipedia, "WP:THREATENING2MEN" only hints at some of the ways in which "power plays" and other practices of exclusion we explore here. However, Bryce's experience is an excellent starting point to think about the complicated ways in which knowledge is deemed relevant on Wikipedia by the "powers" that be, as much of what has been recently illuminated in regard to exclusionary practices on Wikipedia unfortunately falls neatly into his category. However, as with most things, the inclusion issues on Wikipedia remain more convoluted and complicated, and deserve some deeper investigation to untangle the issues. By exploring relevant policies and guidelines, as well as how these are applied (and by whom), we hope to demystify and explain the messiness of these processes.

Untangling the web of practices for what gets included on Wikipedia begins with understanding how the community has set out guidelines and policies for itself. Despite some vagueness in language interpretation and issues arising with the implementation (more on this later) which can (and has) lead to inclusion issues, Notability and its subsequent subpages lay out fairly detailed tests to determine whether a topic or person is deserving of its own page. Notability guidelines are fairly robust, and there are numerous policies that exemplify and limit what can be included as a mainspace page. However, the practices of inclusion and exclusion outside of Notability, such as what to include within a Wikipedia article, remain fairly vague. What is relevant to include *within* an article is often decided (somewhat) arbitrarily by editors, as a project namespace Wikipedia essay[10] entitled "Wikipedia: What to Include" states simply that Wikipedia "should include those facts that are of historical, societal, scientific, intellectual or academic significance."[11] In typical Wikipedia fashion (as the "Wiki" portion of Wikipedia is the linking to other portions of the encyclopedia) the essay refers to two more essays, "Wikipedia:Scope" (WP:SCOPE)[12] and "Wikipedia:What Wikipedia is Not" (WP:NOT),[13] both which help shed light on the practices that construct Wikipedia, but also help ground a broader sense of how Wikipedia consistently defines itself through exclusion and sets up a system that can be easily (power) played to exclude more than is necessary.

What Wikipedia Is Not

Arguably one of Wikipedia's most important policies, particularly when it comes to defining itself, remains "What Wikipedia is not." Originally created in September of 2001, the founding year of Wikipedia, it lays out limits to what Wikipedia should be through what it "is not." Much has changed through time, but the policy attempts to clarify the scope of Wikipedia through excluding certain types of content, interactions with the content, and community behaviors. There are three areas, containing 18 statements of what Wikipedia is *not*, followed by definitions of each of these.[14]

1 Style and format
  - 1.1 Wikipedia is not a paper encyclopedia

2 Encyclopedic content
  - 2.1 Wikipedia is not a dictionary
  - 2.2 Wikipedia is not a publisher of original thought
  - 2.3 Wikipedia is not a soapbox or means of promotion
  - 2.4 Wikipedia is not a mirror or a repository of links, images, or media files
  - 2.5 Wikipedia is not a blog, web hosting service, social networking service, or memorial site
  - 2.6 Wikipedia is not a directory
  - 2.7 Wikipedia is not a manual, guidebook, textbook, or scientific journal
  - 2.8 Wikipedia is not a crystal ball
  - 2.9 Wikipedia is not a newspaper
  - 2.10 Wikipedia is not an indiscriminate collection of information
  - 2.11 Wikipedia is not censored

3 Community
  - 3.1 Wikipedia is not anarchy or a forum for free speech
  - 3.2 Wikipedia is not a democracy

3.3 Wikipedia is not a bureaucracy
3.4 Wikipedia is not a laboratory
3.5 Wikipedia is not a battleground
3.6 Wikipedia is not compulsory

Some of the more important of these lie in defining Wikipedia from news, social media, marketing materials, primary source publishing, and other collections of information. The community guidelines also go so far as to explain (almost ironically considering some of the ways in which members of the community have behaved) that Wikipedia is not a "battleground" to "carry on ideological battles, or nurture prejudice, hatred, or fear." That being said, many of these statements about what Wikipedia "is not" make perfect sense – as it is an encyclopedia (albeit not a paper one), which has its own epistemological foundations as well as a known style and tone that Wikipedia attempts to mirror in many ways.

However, the differences between what Wikipedia "is not" and what Wikipedia "is" are fairly nuanced. Although "Wikipedia is not a mirror or a repository of links, images, or media files," Wikipedia does have an enormous repository of links, and its sister site, Wikimedia Commons (which hosts all of the images on Wikipedia, as well as other things), is, quite specifically, a repository of images and media files. In this case Wikipedia only links and shows the images and files relevant to articles in mainspace, but the difference here is key. Wikipedia might not be a newspaper, but it does aggregate the information of many recent news stories. In this case, Wikipedia remains a tertiary source, but it seeks to collect and aggregate knowledge from the secondary (often newspaper) sources - it relies on, aggregates, and redistributes, but does not *report on*. Wikipedia might not be an "indiscriminate collection of information," but its lofty goal is to collect "the sum of all human knowledge," which not only begs the question "what is not human knowledge?" but also illustrates how Wikipedia answers this and defines "what counts" as knowledge (an argument ripe for debate and conflict on Wikipedia and elsewhere). Finally, although Wikipedia "is not censored" insofar as limiting access to scientific facts and information that some teachers or parents might not want kids to read, it does in fact censor itself through these, and other, exclusionary practices. Each of these differences are slight, but important to consider and recognize that the nuances must both be understood and argued when it comes to *enacting* policy and guidelines. Much like the numerous policies and guidelines that Peake refers to, these nuances can (and have) been utilized as "power plays" that capitalize on these differences when content does not agree with the editor's idea of what should (and should not) be included in Wikipedia.

Since there is no accurate and real way to know the *true* motivations behind editorial exclusions (one could argue that even the editors themselves might not even know), instead of guessing how these editors feel about topics that are, as Peake puts it "WP:-THREATENING2MEN," we can instead turn to exploring how policies, guidelines, and how they have been applied by editors work in the context of a larger system of biases. Essentially, how Wikipedia's editors end up reflecting, amplifying, and funneling biases are often hidden by policies and guidelines, and understanding these processes help to illuminate these extra-exclusionary practices. With this in mind, let us return to the complex guidelines that comprise what Wikipedia defines as "Notability" and its subsequent and related pages, so as to better understand how guideline power is used (and abused) to define what topics and persons deserve their own Wikipedia mainspace page.

Notability: A (Messy) Recipe for Inclusion

Wikipedia's "General notability guideline" (GNG) calls for "significant coverage" in "reliable" and "independent" sources to meet the standards for inclusion in the encyclopedia as a stand-alone article.[15] Each of these terms warrants pages upon pages of discussion within Wikipedia's (numerous) guideline and policy pages. In typical Wiki-fashion, these terms not only link to other guideline pages, but different defining pieces of the terms are also linked. In summation, the GNG expects that any stand-alone article has multiple sources that are (1) considered reliable by consensus of the community,[16] (2) significantly cover the subject itself (not a passing mention), and (3) are independently published from the subject (e.g., press releases, autobiographies, or other coverage directly linked to the subject). However, the GNG goes on to also define a term we might as well have passed over, "presumed," as "coverage in reliable sources creates an assumption, not a guarantee, that a subject merits its own article." This "assumption" creates a space for exclusion beyond the stated guidelines, referring further to "What Wikipedia is Not" (more on this later in the chapter), and opening up space for further whittling down the information included within the encyclopedia.

As is the case with most of Wikipedia's policies and guidelines, there are pages upon pages of guidelines that deal with specifics around how to engage different subjects. In particular, the notability guidelines for people is even more specific than the GNG, breaking down into even smaller sub-categories such as Academics, Creative Professionals, Crime victims and perpetrators, Entertainers, Military personnel, Politicians and judges, and Sports personalities.[17] These guidelines become even more specific for living persons, insisting that "material about living persons added to any Wikipedia page must be written with the greatest care and attention to verifiability, neutrality, and avoidance of original research," and beginning the page with "We must get the article *right*."[18] It is understandable, to a large degree even, the care that is insisted be taken when writing about living people by the guideline, as egregious violations of this policy could easily result in a host of issues of misrepresentation and tabloid-like issues. However, these policies and guidelines that exclude, even rightfully so, a variety of people due to perceived violation of the guidelines, also have been called upon to exclude quite a few notable people, particularly glaringly (and notably due to its increased coverage in independent, secondary, reliable sources) is the exclusion and deletion of women scientists.

Notability and the Case of Clarice Phelps

Although the issues surrounding notability and inclusion of information on Wikipedia are not limited to one area or topic, one of the most visible and widely reported aspects of this representation has been that of biographies of female scientists. Donna Strickland was just one of many, prompting the question "Female scientists' pages keep disappearing from Wikipedia – what's going on?" from *Chemistryworld.com* in 2019.[19] Claire Jarvis, writing for *Fast Company* joins this query, going so far as to call the systemic biases and the apparent exclusion of women Wikipedia's "biggest problem."[20]

A story that may help shed light on Wikipedia's "female scientist problem" is that of Clarice Phelps' page. As an undergraduate, Phelps was part of the Oak Ridge National Laboratory team that discovered *Tennessine*, without a doubt an historic and significant accomplishment by any stretch of the imagination. As part of this team, Phelps has been lauded as the first African-American woman scientist in history to help discover a chemical element. Despite this incredible achievement and press about her accomplishment, Phelps' Wikipedia page was not deemed notable enough to persist for very long, and was deleted on February 11, 2019 after a "brief but intense dispute."[21]

As Jarvis notes,

> ordinarily, such editorial spats are considered a feature of the crowdsourced encyclopedia, not a bug. If one of the site's hundreds of thousands[22] of active contributors mistakenly or purposely adds incorrect information, the wisdom of the crowd will ensure that truth prevails.[23]

Jarvis hits on something important here – it is expected that editorial disagreements are not merely "spats" but instead barriers and gatekeepers that help limit misinformation and overinclusion. The issue here is that the "feature" that helps to limit the garbage on Wikipedia also can be exploited to exclude important information under the guise that editors believe, for one reason or another, such content does not meet the standards of Notability.

This "brief but intense dispute" regarding Phelps' notability refers to Wikipedia's decision-making process, known as "community consensus." Consensus remains a slightly misleading term, as it refers to the outcome of a debate on a topic of concern on Wikipedia, and not some radical process where everyone agrees. It is Wikipedia's system for decision-making, and affects all of the ways that many of these "spats" (and other discussions) are arbitrated. Per the policy page:

> *Consensus* on Wikipedia does not mean unanimity (which is ideal but not always achievable), nor is it the result of a vote. Decision making and reaching consensus involve an effort to incorporate all editors' legitimate concerns, while respecting Wikipedia's policies and guidelines.[24]

In essence, editors are given space and time to discuss (in a series of threaded-style posts and replies) their opinions about a community concern (whether to delete something, to change a policy, or elsewise), and an administrator takes stock of these discussions in an attempt to employ and reflect these concerns into the enactment of a decision on this concern.

Consensus is, by design, a fundamentally messy process, and, whether by design or not, a double-edged sword (or both a feature and a bug, as Jarvis mentions above) as it invites everyone to air their concerns and argue for appropriate application of policy, but at the same time also requires an enormous amount of effort, understanding, and labor on behalf of the participants. The process requires that the user be familiar with the policies of Wikipedia and be willing to and have time to (and care enough to) make policy arguments on behalf of one side or another, as well as know that the argument is taking place at all. The percentage of users who edit Wikipedia is already extremely small, and those familiar with the depth of policy required to participate in these arguments remains far, far smaller.

Phelps' notability was fairly controversial and went through a significant amount of deliberation, including multiple deletion reviews.[25] The page was deleted and restored multiple times over the previous year before its February 11 AfD (or "Article for deletion") decision, with an incredible amount of discussion. The final AfD discussion, ending on February 11, 2020 amounted to over 16,000 words, the equivalent of 64 pages of double-spaced text. The intense debate over Phelps' notability, particularly around whether she had received significant coverage (many argued she did not, but even so pointed that the issue of this coverage remained a symptom of systemic biases). However, in the end, after numerous deliberations as well as an arbitration, her page was restored and editors continued its improvement, where it persists to this day. The process "worked" insofar as the page was eventually restored and improved, but in the end this process exacted huge amounts of labor from the volunteer community and may not have been restored if not for it being called out in other venues for issues of representation and bias.

We could argue that this is just a blip that is part of a larger process to retrain editorial bias, and that better policy will ensure better inclusion. However, Phelps' page was nominated for AfD by an anonymous IP address (an unregistered editor). Thousands of words, countless hours of discussion both on and off Wikipedia, press coverage, and rounds of review and arbitration later, all because of an anonymous nomination for deletion. However, with such epic efforts necessary to preserve this one page, the process itself must come into question – how do anonymous editors hold so much power? At first glance, it seems important that editors can nominate articles for deletion, but when anonymous editors can shine a spotlight onto a new(ish) page (before improvements can be made) that kicks off a process requiring hundreds of hours of volunteer labor, the process seems lacking some basic stop-gaps, especially when the requirements for participation remain so high. Instead of an egalitarian process of "anyone can edit," these types of deletionist tactics end up as "power plays" where editors can exert their power of expertise by changing the game – ensuring that pages undergo a complicated bureaucratic process that the average Wikipedia user not only does not understand, but is often not even aware exists. Of course, these "power plays" tend to play out more often on articles about people, places, and things that are traditionally underrepresented, which ensures that those arguing for exclusion are often "backed up" by the Notability policy due to larger systemic issues of representation. If it was not completely obvious by now, the most glaringly obvious exclusion on Wikipedia remains that of women.

Jarvis is not alone in the concern over "Wikipedia's biggest problem," as many have noted the exclusion of women from the encyclopedia as a glaring concern. WikiProject[26] Women in Red (WiR), a reference to how red links on Wikipedia signify a missing page (as opposed to blue which link to an existing page), was founded in July 2015 to increase the representation of women on Wikipedia. According to WiR "in October 2014, only 15.53% of English Wikipedia's biographies were about women," but with the help of WiR and others concerned about this gender and content gap, that percentage has increased to 18.64% as of 20 November 2020.[27] There are at least two pieces to understanding this significant increase in representation, one lies in the attention that women's biographies have received amongst editors and authors of Wikipedia pages – quite simply, people are aware of the issues and focusing on writing more biographies on women. The second, as we have discussed with Phelps and Strickland's pages, is that this attention also has made clear the issues with deletionist tendencies toward pages that, even if they might not be perfect, were notable and deserving of improvement.

As with most things, Wikipedia has an extensive page explaining AfD, as well as an extensive deletion policy. Under the header "Nominating article(s) for deletion" the first subheading is "Before nominating: checks and alternatives," (this is also known as WP:BEFORE) in which the page specifically asks editors to: Read and understand a series of policies and guidelines, carry out a series of checks, consider whether the article could be improved rather than deleted, and search for additional sources, if the main concern is notability.[28] Quite specifically, the recommendation for editors is to nominate for deletion only as a last resort, even after doing additional research to improve the article. Running counter to experiences regarding Phelps and Stricklands' pages, this recommendation underscores the difference between how power plays can "play out" and the intention of policy that seeks to preserve good content and protect against garbage, as well as highlights the frustrations and tensions between these ways of handling content.

WiR has their own informational essay about how to deal with the frustrations of addressing the representation issue on Wikipedia, stating

> If an article you have written is declined at articles for creation (AfC), nominated for deletion (AfD), or proposed for deletion (PROD), don't panic or get angry. Take time to improve the article, ask for help and participate in the discussion.[29]

The essay explains a myriad of reasons for why an article might have been rejected (or potentially rejected) in one form or another. What is notable about the article and its advice is that it is incredibly sober about recommendations for editors facing (understandably) frustrating situations. Wikipedia's policies and guidelines are meticulously explained, and, in particular, the essay stresses how to work within the system, to be patient, continue to improve articles, and to reach out for assistance when needed. Even the organization that was founded specifically to address systemic issues within Wikipedia addresses the issues with what seems to be similar manner as the section in the AfD project namespace entitled "Before nominating: checks and alternatives" (WP:BEFORE) which stresses that one should continue to work diligently, patiently, kindly, and within the parameters and guidelines that have been agreed on (by consensus) and laid out on Wikipedia. It seems that the community, at least what is written by the community and those involved in the consensus on policies and guidelines, is all on the same page. How then, might there be so many issues with representation on Wikipedia, particularly in regard to deleting pages of women?

The story of Clarice Phelps' page is interesting for multiple reasons that help to highlight what we argue are more endemic to Wikipedia than simply the exclusion of particular people or topics, as Phelps ends up not just a story about the deletion of a black female scientist, but a story of the incredible amount of labor and struggle involved to argue for notability when the spotlight is turned on.

Wikipedia pages evolve over time, adding new information and citations to improve articles. Many articles begin as stubs, with very little information. Phelps' page, albeit somewhat underdeveloped at the time, was still undergoing evolution. The difference here is that her page came under extreme scrutiny while still in its infancy due to some (anonymous) editor deciding it needed immediate addressing (for deletion). In Phelps' case, it seems that the policies and guidelines "worked," as in that the guidelines for Notability and the policies regarding AfD, deletion review, and arbitration ended up preserving her page. So it is not the policies that are "broken" here, but instead we should ask why was this such a difficult and extensive case, where many other pages are not put under such an extreme spotlight?

As with many things on Wikipedia, the intention of the policies are "in good faith" and are meant to be applied as such. In a perfect world, Phelps' page would have not been nominated for deletion at all, but instead (as recommended by the AfD policy page) the editor who found the page lacking would have done the due diligence to seek out new sources and improve the article themselves rather than nominating it for deletion. However, recommendations and guidelines are not always applied equally or in "good faith" by all, as Wikipedia is edited by volunteers, many of them anonymous or pseudonymous, and all of which (other than the bots, of course) are human, and suffer from biases, whether they acknowledge them or not.

Beyond Policies: Exclusion through Other Means

Although Wikipedia's community and its critics are both well aware of Wikipedia's "systemic bias" issues, many toss the term around quite a bit, often obfuscating the complex layers of meaning that the term implies. To make sense of how information is included (or excluded) from Wikipedia, it is important to understand how these "systemic biases" operate throughout the lifecycle of information, and how Wikipedia both participates in this "system" as well as how the community attempts to combat these biases through practices and policies.

The "systemic" part of "systemic biases" is often the most overlooked portion of the term, as it refers how these biases manifest throughout a complex system and not the "fault" of any one particular person, policy, group, organization, or otherwise. Wikipedia is, as we discuss throughout this book, an incredibly complex system, in conversation and reliant on numerous other complex systems as it seeks to represent "the sum of all human knowledge." Wikipedia can be considered both a perpetrator and victim of bias as it exists within the system of information as well as attempts to represent this sum of human knowledge.

At the time of this writing, Wikipedia's own entry on "Systemic bias" defines the phenomenon as "the inherent tendency of a process to support particular outcomes."[30] The article goes on to explain issues around cognitive biases in human-centered processes and how issues around racism, sexism, and other discriminatory perceptions influence outcomes in a system, even if the participants are not aware of it. In essence, a systemic bias exists when a particular outcome is influenced heavily through a variety of means which manifest a predisposition for a specific result. A "stacked deck" but not just one stacked deck, but instead a series of stacked decks which ensure a precise outcome. As with most stacked decks, it is often impossible to understand how these issues manifest without looking for larger patterns. Systemic biases are a result of unchecked cognitive biases that people, often unwittingly, continue to allow to influence their behavior. Whether sexism, racism, or other perceptions, these cognitive biases influence the editorial and writing decisions on Wikipedia, of course, but also influence the focus of researchers, historians, journalists, and other producers of information and knowledge. Because of Wikipedia's reliance on secondary sources, systemic biases have the potential to be magnified within the encyclopedia, as Wikipedia suffers from both its own systemic bias influenced human-centered processes, and relies on other sources suffering from systemic biases. Biases beget biases, which then beget more biases, further moving the needle further and further away from any resemblance of fair or equitable. Instead of thinking about systemic bias as simply a cognitive bias that excludes those not in power, let us break down a variety of particular ways how what gets included in Wikipedia is often influenced and limited by a variety of systemic biases.

Systemic biases are historically sexist, racist, and Eurocentric. This is not (necessarily) an overt thing, but a product of both the cognitive biases of those who control what is published, and those doing the writing itself. As discussed in Chapter 2, Wikipedia's reliance on print culture remains a major potential area for biases as not only are printed sources historically exclusionary of non-Western and oral histories, but the historic control of the printed word itself has also been limited. Throughout most of history the vast majority of the written word has been controlled, through a variety of means, by a very limited demographic. Namely this demographic consists of white, male, educated, European and North Americans. Women, non-Europeans, non-whites, and less educated people not only had severely limited access to publishing, but they also were limited in representation by those who were controlling the printing. This is, of course, widely understood and known – the history of the printed word is not very long, and has for much of its time been controlled by very few. However, it is important to understand that much of the history of knowledge, that which is the grist for which Wikipedia is built on, is already tainted by biases, ensuring that the representation of topics within Wikipedia will suffer heavily from this bias, regardless of how neutral Wikipedia's editors may (or may not) be. The equitable representation of all of history cannot be fully possible as much knowledge has certainly been lost or just gone uncaptured by secondary sources.

Of course, cognitive biases still persist today in the production of secondary sources. The inequitable coverage of women scientists reflects only a small portion of the ways in which representation by journalists fails to capture the depth and breadth of a diverse and multicultural world. Cognitive biases persist amongst those who write and publish in academia and in journalism – and this is not any singular person's responsibility (as one cannot write about what one does not know about). Instead, the system which continues to enable these issues must be held accountable, and in many ways it has. In recent years, many of these issues have been exposed and not only has there been great strides and improvements in Wikipedia, but a light has been cast on the issues persistent throughout journalism and academia as well. There is a long road ahead, but it appears (and hopes) to include more diverse and representative voices and stories. Of course, it is regretful it has taken so long as so much has been lost and passed, never to be captured again due to the long tail of these biases.

Amplification and the "Funneling" of Biases in Wikipedia

In the end, editors are volunteers, and that type of labor must be met with a lot of consideration for how information is produced on Wikipedia. The functional complexities of volunteer labor is something that many non-Wikipedians, particularly those who have covered some of these issues with representation and inclusion on Wikipedia, often ignore (or at least do not fully explore) the larger effects of. On a very basic level, it is important to consider that editors are not paid for what they are writing and instead are motivated by other means. Volunteers write Wikipedia, and are not necessarily motivated by information representation as social justice (at least insofar as in reaction to systemic biases), and insisting that a volunteer write about things that they are not necessarily interested in might end up antithetical to the type of attitude that encourages volunteers to write a general knowledge encyclopedia to give away online for free.

As mentioned in Chapter 1, online communities, especially ones that allow pseudonymous participation, are notoriously hard to measure demographically. A few studies have been attempted on Wikipedia which can give insight into the composition of the community, which are catalogued and summarized in the project namespace page Wikipedia:Wikipedians (or WP:User).[31] Statistics and demographics might not tell the whole story, but they can at least begin to paint a picture of the shape and size of the community that creates Wikipedia, and offer some clues into contextualizing some of the concerns.

Of the 40+ million users, only about 130k users are active on average. Although only about %0.05 of "users" actually participate in the community, Wikipedia's community is incredibly large, with over 40 million registered editors.[32] However, compared to billions of views on Wikipedia, only about 130k editors are active (more than one edit in the past month) each month.[33] The average user, according to these studies, is male (84%), resides in the US (20%) or Germany (12%), are aged between 17 and 40 (59%), primarily edit (79%) and read (49%) the English Wikipedia. Users on average are highly educated, as they have completed high school (30%), a bachelors or associate degree (35%), a masters (18%), or a PhD (8%). Most (66%) of editors state that most of their volunteer activity is spent editing existing articles, while 28% created new articles as their primary activity. There are no reported demographics on racial makeup.

Wikipedian motivation is also fairly straightforward, as far as a 2011 editor survey suggests, as 71% of editors like the idea of sharing knowledge, and 69% of editors believe that "information should be freely available." Unsurprisingly, as people (especially volunteers) like to do things they enjoy, 63% of editors are motivated by the prospect of contributing what they believe that they have expertise in.[34]

The average editor of Wikipedia is not at all representative of the world's population by any stretch of the imagination. Although a fairly narrow demographic to represent "the sum of all human knowledge," understanding the population and motivations of Wikipedians helps to bring context to the volunteer group populating this massive knowledge base. These volunteers, who might have started off writing about South Park, Pokemon, or World War II Battleships, are the base population that then can potentially be promoted to administrative positions within the volunteer community. Editors, whether they admit it or not, may carry editorial biases to administrative positions, and those who "stuck around long enough" then go on to make larger decisions about inclusion of information within Wikipedia. More of this in Chapter 4, but this is why it remains imperative to understand who continues to be invited in versus who feels excluded from the community, as the pipeline for all volunteer projects, especially Wikipedia, is incredibly leaky – especially so for underrepresented groups. This all being said, some volunteers are precisely motivated by representation and information as social justice, particularly many new editors and those teaching with Wikipedia, as a survey of instructors teaching Wikipedia assignments found that 40% of participants noted that they wanted to "address an issue of social inequity" as a primary motivation for teaching a Wikipedia-based assignment.[35] What it comes down to is that volunteers have numerous (often unsaid and even unknown) motivations for contributing, and understanding this is key to encouraging new, diverse editorship with diverse interests.

What we can surmise from this is not that Wikipedia editors are not necessarily consciously (at least for the most part) contributing to the gap of issues of coverage and representation within Wikipedia. However, when understood in a larger system of decision-making and how cognitive biases manifest *unconsciously*, we can understand how the human-centered and community-based system of authorship and editing on Wikipedia, as Katherine Maher points out, can (and often does) reflect (and even magnify) the biases that already exist in the larger information landscape. This is not to say that Wikipedia is "bad" or that editors are "bad" (although there are definitely instances of bad actors on Wikipedia). Instead, these issues bring into context how this amazing community that built this incredible wonder of modern society also succumbs to and participates in perpetuating information biases that often ignore underrepresented groups and continues to marginalize non-white, non-male, non-Western ideas, subjects, and people.

This helps bring focus and context for many issues of the gender gap, exclusion, and topical bias on Wikipedia. In the end, it only takes one bad actor to suggest deleting a page, focusing the spotlight on one article over another, while cognitive biases multiply through Wikipedia, amplifying the issues of coverage in the larger world to continue to exclude certain topics and people. Understanding this complex problem helps us to think about how to shift perspectives on inclusion criteria and notability, particularly for living persons.

However, even if one was to wave a magic wand and somehow fix all of Wikipedia's bias issues (and for that matter, the world's biases, as Wikipedia's representation of reality is shaped by world's secondary sources), there would still be the matter of *access* to sources so that the editors can continue to collect and disseminate the world's knowledge. Not only must the secondary sources actually *cover* all of these topics and people, but these sources must be accessible to editors to find and read them in the first place. Furthermore, they should be accessible to future editors so that the information can be verifiable.

Unequal Access to Sources

Wikipedia's grand mission to collect and freely distribute the "sum of all human knowledge" is not only incredibly vast and grand, its ethos also runs counter to the accessibility (and copyright) of much of the information it is trying to distribute. Wikipedia is what many refer to as an "open access" resource, which means that it is free to access by anyone, and functions under what is called a "Creative Commons Attribution/Share-Alike 3.0 Unported License" (CC-BY-SA). CC-BY-SA goes beyond just the ability to access, however, and grants that Wikipedia is free to not only access by anyone, but also to distribute, copy, and even sell copies of, as long as the distributor maintains both the attribution and the licensing (this is the "share alike" portion).[36]

However, as Wikipedia is a tertiary source and relies upon secondary sources to back up its claims, Wikipedia must link to or reference each and every statement made on Wikipedia.[37] This presents (at least) two major problems. The first is simply that access is unequal across different users, as many important sources of secondary information (particularly academic journals but also many newspapers) lie behind often cost-prohibitive paywalls. This can limit editors' ability to improve articles, particularly when trying to address knowledge gaps that already are underrepresented in secondary literature. Second, this can create serious problems for accessing the "grist" for Wikipedia if it is not also open access. If each statement must be verifiable, it should be verifiable by "every single person on the planet" if Wikipedia is to be truly "open access" – or else how can Wikipedia ensure that the information is verifiably correct? This ensures that there are perpetually "tiers" of access to knowledge and representation of knowledge, where many editors cannot actually verify the knowledge re-presented in Wikipedia.

On top of all this, even academic libraries are running into issues accessing information (sometimes even authored by their own faculty). Due to bundling practices by academic journals (which force libraries to purchase licenses for multiple journals at a time to get access to the highest referenced ones) journals can charge libraries ever increasing fees for their subscriptions. This situation has collectively been dubbed the "Serial Crisis" as library budgets have become overrun by these increasing costs.[38] So profound is this "crisis" that one of the most well-funded universities in the world, Harvard University, has stated that it cannot continue to afford publisher's prices.[39] This leads to significant issues for access for *anyone,* even those with the privileges of an academic institution. That of course, assumes the information is available in the first place.

Wikipedia's mission to collect and distribute all the world's knowledge comes up against a major setback due to its reliance on secondary sources. As mentioned before, there is and always has been a significant lack of coverage in general for many topics and people, particularly outside of the Western world. The system of information that Wikipedia relies upon privileges written knowledge, which leaves out an incredible amount of the world's "knowledge."

As discussed in Chapter 2, the encyclopedia's policy for verifiability, while a key element in the construction of reliability, limits its capacity for representing global knowledge. Not all knowledge exists in written, published form, yet Wikipedia continues to adhere to print culture to verify factual claims. The logocentric reliance on written knowledge privileges certain cultures with a long tradition of print-based knowledge curation, while marginalizing others. Indigenous cultures that rely on oral history to pass down knowledge, for instance, cannot be adequately represented according to Wikipedia's verifiability policies. Peter Gallert and Maja Van der Velden have described this particular circumstance as "Wikipedia's Catch-22."[40] Wikipedia builds its reputation upon print-centric policies such as verifiability to ensure reliability in the encyclopedia, yet those exact policies also limit the encyclopedia's capacity to achieve universal coverage of knowledge due to its exclusion of other forms of knowledge capture.

To address these issues, there have been a few projects to seek out and replace paywalled links, as well as for editors to help provide access to others. There was even a potential project at one point to investigate how to make space for oral histories, particularly to capture knowledge from historically underrepresented (and under-documented) areas.[41] However, much like many of the policies, guidelines, and procedures on Wikipedia, these situations, projects, and "solutions" are palliative treatments to systemic problems that are fundamental to how Wikipedia functions.

This is all to say that Wikipedia's grand vision of capturing and distributing the world's knowledge is at odds with numerous barriers from the information itself. Stuart Brand famously declared that information "wants to be free,"[42] a much lauded and celebrated phrase during the techno-utopian, early Internet days. However, in the end much information is not free, and any project that seeks free (access of) information (such as Wikipedia) must wrestle with the complex issues posed by the realities of information access.

The answer to how Wikipedia decides on what gets included is simply "people," although obviously a bit more complicated when issues of consensus-based decision-making, policies, and guidelines are further confused by cognitive biases and gatekeeping editors. Compounded with increasing issues around subscription-based paywalled information and historic systemic biases in the production of secondary information, Wikipedia's potential for inclusion regarding topics and information is greatly limited by accessibility and availability of information, which significantly limits Wikipedia's capacity for decision-making about information and its ability to fulfil its grand promise.

Who Really Decides and Why?

Throughout this chapter, we have discussed the ways in which Wikipedia decides what gets included, which, in the end, amounts to how Wikipedia decides what counts as "knowledge" worthy of inclusion in the "sum of all human knowledge." Building on how Wikipedia constructs its version of "truth" and "facts" through its policy of reliability, the policy of Notability, among other policies and guidelines (WP:NOT, WP:BEYOND, AfD, etc.) that interact with it, constitute the major frameworks for how Wikipedia decides what counts as knowledge, and from that knowledge, how reality is represented.

Wikipedia's policies and construction are just one piece of the puzzle here, as not only is the sum total of potential "knowledge" limited by historically biased information, but biases persist in many ways in the construction of knowledge. Wikipedia is, in effect, plagued by its own policy of reliability as it outsources its trust in information in those who have the power to publish. Reliability on Wikipedia becomes a double-edged sword when it fails to count as notable knowledge due to current and historical biases. Despite its best efforts, there always remains a gap between the *actuality* of reality and the potential for Wikipedia to represent it.

Finally, Wikipedia's editors not only cannot combat the larger systemic biases (as they can only represent what has been written), but also suffer their own biases in the decision-making that finalizes what gets included in "the sum of all human knowledge." Whether "in good faith" or not, Wikipedia's editors are (mostly) human and will always suffer some biases, whether they recognize it or not. This could be mitigated, of course, through stronger guidelines and policies, but when a single anonymous editor can prompt hundreds of hours of labor from dozens of editors just to debate whether an article should remain on mainspace, it seems that the current guidelines and policies are not robust enough to ensure an equitable space. The techno-utopian ideals of Wikipedia, particularly "Assume Good Faith" are wonderful in theory, but in practice not only allow for deletionist practices that obscure the sexist and racist biases of some editors but award these editors with incredible power to control what gets included on Wikipedia. When significant *real life human women* are denied coverage, but every *Pokémon* and *Family Guy* character have their own page, something might be awry.

In the end, Wikipedia is a community, and the community decides what gets included. Understanding and questioning how the community comes together, how it functions, and how it is changing will help bring together a holistic understanding of Wikipedia's past, present, and its future as it continues on its grand mission to represent our reality. In the following chapter, we will explore and question the various aspects of the community both on and offline, and how it both continues the mission as well as attempts to look forward to how it must shape itself, and therefore shape Wikipedia, in the future.

Notes

1 "Wikipedia: Notability," Wikipedia, last modified December 20, 2020, https://en.wikipedia.org/w/index.php?title=Wikipedia:Notability&oldid=995288718.
2 Ibid.
3 "The New York Times," Wikipedia, last modified December 2, 2020, https://en.wikipedia.org/w/index.php?title=The_New_York_Times&oldid=991895613.
4 Katherine Maher, Twitter Post, "Journalists — If You're Going to Come after @Wikipedia for It's Coverage of Women…" Twitter, October 3, 2018, https://twitter.com/krmaher/status/1047453672790093824.
5 Roblimo, "Wikipedia Founder Jimmy Wales Responds," *Slashdot* (blog), last modified July 28, 2004, https://slashdot.org/story/04/07/28/1351230/wikipedia-founder-jimmy-wales-responds.
6 We use the term deletionist or deletionism to describe an editorial predilection to remove rather than add content to the encyclopedia mainspace.
7 Bryce Peake, "WP:THREATENING2MEN:Misogynist Infopolitics and the Hegemony of the Asshole Consensus on English Wikipedia," *ADA, A Journal of Gender, New Media, and Technology* 7 (April 2015). https://adanewmedia.org/2015/04/issue7-peake/.
8 Ibid.
9 Travis Kriplean, Ivan Beschastnikh, David W. McDonald, and Scott A. Golder, "Community, Consensus, Coercion, Control: Cs*w or How Policy Mediates Mass Participation," in *Proceedings of the 2007 International ACM Conference on Supporting Group Work*, Sanibel Island, Florida, USA, (2007): 167–176, https://doi.org/10.1145/1316624.1316648.
10 As discussed in Chapter 1, Wikipedia's project namespace contains numerous policies, guidelines, and even essays on how to write Wikipedia, how to conduct oneself in Wikipedia, and a variety of other topics. They

are part of Wikipedia but not the "mainspace" that constitutes the encyclopedia, but instead contains numerous pages that provide tips, examples, and guidelines on how to best create and maintain Wikipedia.

11 Wikipedia: What to Include," Wikipedia, last modified August 16, 2019, https://en.wikipedia.org/w/index.php?title=Wikipedia:What_to_include&oldid=911131538.

12 "Wikipedia: Scope," Wikipedia, last modified May 20, 2019, https://en.wikipedia.org/w/index.php?title=Wikipedia:Scope&oldid=897922426.

13 "Wikipedia: What Wikipedia Is Not," Wikipedia, last modified July 15, 2020, https://en.wikipedia.org/w/index.php?title=Wikipedia:What_Wikipedia_is_not&oldid=967817887.

14 Ibid.

15 "Wikipedia: Notability," Wikipedia, last modified December 20, 2020, https://en.wikipedia.org/w/index.php?title=Wikipedia:Notability&oldid=995288718.

16 See Chapter 2 for more explanation.

17 "Wikipedia: Notability (People)," Wikipedia, last modified August 23, 2020, https://en.wikipedia.org/w/index.php?title=Wikipedia:Notability_(people)&oldid=974588424.

18 "Wikipedia: Biographies of Living Persons," Wikipedia, last modified October 5, 2020, https://en.wikipedia.org/w/index.php?title=Wikipedia:Biographies_of_living_persons&oldid=981904218.

19 Katrina Kramer, "Female Scientists' Pages Keep Disappearing from Wikipedia – What's Going on?" Chemistry World (webpage), July 3, 2019, https://www.chemistryworld.com/news/female-scientists-pages-keep-disappearing-from-wikipedia-whats-going-on/3010664.article.

20 Claire Jarvis, "A Deleted Wikipedia Page Speaks Volumes about Its Biggest Problem," *Fast Company*, last modified April 25, 2019. https://www.fastcompany.com/90339700/a-deleted-wikipedia-page-speaks-volumes-about-its-biggest-problem.

21 Ibid.

22 As of the time of this writing, there are an average of 131k active editors per month. Active editors are defined as "*Registered* users who have performed an action in the last 30 days; the number of unregistered active users is not compiled" "Wikipedia: Statistics," Wikipedia, last modified October 3, 2020, https://en.wikipedia.org/w/index.php?title=Wikipedia:Statistics&oldid=981585678.

23 Jarvis, "A Deleted Wikipedia Page."

24 "Wikipedia: Consensus," Wikipedia, October 14, 2020, last modified October 14, 2020. https://en.wikipedia.org/w/index.php?title=Wikipedia:Consensus&oldid=983556771.

25 "Wikipedia: Deletion Review/Log/2020 January 31," Wikipedia, last modified February 8, 2020, https://en.wikipedia.org/w/index.php?title=Wikipedia:Deletion_review/Log/2020_January_31&oldid=939731312.

26 WikiProjects are organized groups of editors dedicated to improving a particular subject area or "project" in the encyclopedia.

27 "Wikipedia: WikiProject Women in Red," Wikipedia, last modified November 20, 2020, https://en.wikipedia.org/w/index.php?title=Wikipedia:WikiProject_Women_in_Red&oldid=989654837.

28 "Wikipedia: Articles for Deletion," Wikipedia, last modified November 21, 2020, https://en.wikipedia.org/w/index.php?title=Wikipedia:Articles_for_deletion&oldid=989883288.
29 "Wikipedia: WikiProject Women in Red/Essays/Primer for AfD, AfC and PROD," Wikipedia, last modified September 22, 2020, https://en.wikipedia.org/w/index.php?title=Wikipedia:WikiProject_Women_in_Red/Essays/Primer_for_AfD,_AfC_and_PROD&oldid=979787246.
30 "Systemic Bias," Wikipedia, last modified July 11, 2020, https://en.wikipedia.org/w/index.php?title=Systemic_bias&oldid=967204152.
31 "Wikipedia: Wikipedians," Wikipedia, last modified December 1, 2020, https://en.wikipedia.org/w/index.php?title=Wikipedia:Wikipedians&oldid=991744041.
32 "Wikipedia: Statistics," Wikipedia, last modified October 3, 2020, https://en.wikipedia.org/w/index.php?title=Wikipedia:Statistics&oldid=981585678.
33 Note that "users" represents all of Wikipedia's registered users. This number significantly drops when taking into account user levels based on participation. See section on User Access levels for a breakdown of this.
34 "Wikipedia: Wikipedians."
35 Jiawei Xing and Matthew Vetter. "Editing for Equity: Understanding Instructor Motivations for Integrating Cross-Disciplinary Wikipedia Assignments," *First Monday*, May 25, 2020, https://doi.org/10.5210/fm.v25i6.10575.
36 "Wikipedia: FAQ/Copyright," Wikipedia, last modified August 29, 2020, https://en.wikipedia.org/w/index.php?title=Wikipedia:FAQ/Copyright&oldid=975545050.
37 For more on this, see internal Wikipedia essays such as:
"Wikipedia: You Do Need to Cite That the Sky Is Blue," Wikipedia, last modified June 2, 2020, https://en.wikipedia.org/w/index.php?title=Wikipedia:You_do_need_to_cite_that_the_sky_is_blue&oldid=960389350.
"Wikipedia: Why Most Sentences Should Be Cited," Wikipedia, last modified June 2, 2020, https://en.wikipedia.org/w/index.php?title=Wikipedia:Why_most_sentences_should_be_cited&oldid=960321257.
"Wikipedia: The Pope Is Catholic," Wikipedia, last modified September 6, 2020, https://en.wikipedia.org/w/index.php?title=Wikipedia:The_Pope_is_Catholic&oldid=977052665.
38 Judith M. Panitch and Sarah Michalak, "The Serials Crisis: A White Paper for the UNC-Chapel Hill Scholarly Communications Convocation," accessed December 18, 2020, https://ils.unc.edu/courses/2019_fall/inls700_001/Readings/Panitch2005-SerialsCrisis.htm; Justin Fox, "Academic Publishing Can't Remain Such a Great Business: Free Access to Research Is Coming Someday," November 3, 2015, https://www.bloomberg.com/opinion/articles/2015-11-03/academic-publishing-can-t-remain-such-a-great-business.
39 Ian Sample, "Harvard University Says It Can't Afford Journal Publishers' Prices," The Guardian, April 24, 2012, http://www.theguardian.com/science/2012/apr/24/harvard-university-journal-publishers-prices.
40 Peter Gallert and Maja Van der Velden, "Reliable Sources for Indigenous Knowledge: Dissecting Wikipedia's Catch-22," in Embracing Indigenous

Knowledge in a New Technology Design Paradigm, eds. Nicola J. Bidwell and Heike Winschiers-Theophilus (Indigenous Knowledge Technology Conference, 2013), http://ir.nust.na/jspui/handle/10628/409.

41 This project, unfortunately did not reach fruition. However, other ways of capturing similar types of knowledge have been proposed.

42 R. Polk Wagner, "Information Wants to Be Free: Intellectual Property and the Mythologies of Control," *Columbia Law Review* (2003): 995–1034.

4 How Wikipedia Decides on Who Gets to Contribute

Wikipedia Community and Engagement

> I am supposing that in every society the production of discourse is at once controlled, selected, organised and redistributed according to a certain number of procedures, whose role is to avert its powers and its dangers, to cope with chance events, to evade its ponderous, awesome materiality.
>
> —Michel Foucault, *The Discourse on Language*

Introduction

Although Wikipedia purports to be a place where "the sum of all human knowledge" can be freely composed, collected, and disseminated, those of us who have been involved with the community for any length of time know all too well that in practice the reality does not fully match this utopian vision. As discussed through previous chapters, this mismatch between Wikipedia's vision and the reality of the encyclopedia extends throughout a variety of policies and guidelines when applied in differing ways in the community. What we further explore here are some of the ways the community itself functions as a barrier to its own vision not only through individual actions, but also how it has been set up to fail before it begins due to its fundamental organizing and premises. As we have laid out throughout the book, Wikipedia is, as Foucault notes in the epigraph, "controlled, organi[z]ed and redistributed according to a certain number of procedures" that, in the end, help the community to "cope with" and "evade its ponderous, awesome materiality." These procedures help Wikipedia function but often they also obfuscate the material effects of that system and the community, and therefore the encyclopedia suffers.

DOI: 10.4324/9781003094081-4

As discussed in Chapter 3, Wikipedia, much like many systems, defines itself through exclusion. This is not necessarily a bad thing, as Wikipedia cannot be *everything to everyone*.[1] What things *are not* are often just as important, if not more, as what things are. Differentiation and categorization often rises from exclusion rather than inclusion. The community of Wikipedia understands this, as it needs to constantly push back against the "firehose of misinformation" and maintain the integrity and trustworthiness of Wikipedia. However, in its struggle to maintain its integrity, Wikipedia can turn a blind eye to how and why it chooses to exclude, and the human element that gets either shunned or shies away from the community during the course of this struggle. In this way and others, Wikipedia defines not only the encyclopedia but also its community through exclusion. Wikipedia is not unlike other communities in that it excludes participation from some, while inviting participation from others (then again, it is the only one that also purports to be the encyclopedia *anyone can edit*).

Communities are often exclusionary, and all follow particular rules, those of which are often unsaid but understood. In *The Discourse on Language*, Foucault discusses rules and types of exclusion as a way to understand, beginning with the exclusion of prohibition. He asserts that

> we have three types of prohibition, covering objects, ritual with its surrounding circumstances, the privileged or exclusive right to speak of a particular subject; these prohibitions interrelate, reinforce and complement each other, forming a complex web, continually subject to modification.[2]

What Foucault offers us here is that the rules of societies and communities are governed by prohibition in numerous ways, and these prohibitions overlap and blend to define what is permissible within that community.

Wikipedia is a community, and like any community it is social in numerous ways. Thinking about Wikipedia as a social community enables us not only to understand its various rites and procedures; such a project also allows for a deeper dive into the ways that certain discourses and identities are excluded or "prohibited" within the Wikipedia community. Each aspect of these, whether objects, ritual, or right to speak, all intersect and "interrelate" into how Wikipedia's community polices its boundaries.

First, we can understand "objects" here simply as digital spaces on Wikipedia – pages and words within the encyclopedia and the

Wikipedia project at large. Throughout this book we have discussed plenty of prohibitions and exclusions in this regard, from style, to content, to the interface itself. Second, while "ritual" might seem like an odd term to apply to Wikipedia, we understand the policies and guidelines in Wikipedia as types of rites and rituals, as they are defined customs or practices that the community refers to and polices the use of. How the community communicates (how discourse is managed and policed), whether on talk pages or AfD discussions, are all part of the rituals of Wikipedia's community. An application of Foucault's third type of prohibition can be seen in two different ways, one in regard to user permissions, as well as understanding and mastery of procedure (being able to follow the rituals). The second becomes apparent in that there are spoken and unspoken norms and practices in Wikipedia that actively prohibit or exclude certain individuals from engaging in the Wikipedia community. We have attempted to make visible many of the invisible, unstated, or otherwise obfuscated norms and rituals that govern how Wikipedia works. Following this archaeological approach in regard to exclusion and prohibition, we explore how the community operates in a similar way – that policies and/or actions of the community empower some voices while excluding others (the ways in which are often obfuscated by the community's techno-optimistic and enlightenment rhetoric).

This chapter explores the ways in which the Wikipedia community (the community which both maintains the encyclopedia as well as decides on how it will be maintained) regulates and polices itself both actively and passively through its practices. Drawing from Foucault's discussion of exclusion and prohibition through his definition of exclusion we take to heart the relationship between power and production of discourse and recognize these prohibitive practices as part of the "power plays" discussed in Chapter 3. Beyond just the content, these practices exclude and police participation within the community, the same one which then turns to creating and policing the content – controlling and policing who creates the content in turn makes great strides toward controlling and policing the content. As the community that controls the largest repository of human knowledge on earth, how this community polices itself and how these exclusionary practices play out are imperative to understand, as they have direct consequences on how knowledge is accumulated and stored on Wikipedia.

Through exploring some examples of how this plays out in the community we will tease out some of the larger issues that have plagued Wikipedia's community for years. These issues, which are not news at all to most Wikipedians, will be examined as part of a larger systemic issue through an exploration of the foundations of Wikipedia and the community assumptions and practices that helped to create what Wikipedia became. This will give space to critique some of the policies and practices, and examine some of the practices that the community has engaged to combat some of its issues.

Exclusion in the Wikipedia Community

We explore three specific types of participation exclusion occurring in Wikipedia's community that have been documented by researchers studying the intersection of participation and the social and cultural politics of exclusion within the encyclopedia's community.[3] Often overlapping, the ways in which participation is excluded on Wikipedia is not always cut and dry – however, broadly categorized, they fall within varying levels of gender (and race) based harassment, extra labor, and gatekeeping newcomers. Furthermore, it is important to note that all of these practices discussed are types of harassing behavior in that, whether consciously intended or not, serve to create an unwelcoming and exclusive environment for the potential participants. Whether overt (blatant harassment) or somewhat covert (gatekeeping), prohibitive practices by the community create and reinforce the space of Wikipedia as exclusionary, despite its "open door" policy.

Gatekeeping Newcomers

As both instructors that often teach with Wikipedia as well as volunteers at Wikipedia edit-a-thons, we have experience with introducing hundreds of newcomers to the ins and outs of Wikipedia. Even when led through the process by a seasoned veteran Wikipedia can be daunting, but time and time again the biggest setbacks to new editors has been dealing with the community. Despite being the encyclopedia "anyone can edit," Wikipedia has a reputation, even amongst the community, as an unwelcome space for newcomers. As one seasoned editor explains, "We throw brand new potential editors directly into shark infested waters, then yell at them for splashing at the sharks."[4] Despite being told not to "bite the newcomers," unfortunately the editors on Wikipedia often bite, particularly those who are "thrown in" and are already struggling with trying to swim.

The initial excitement of writing for a global online platform can dissipate quickly when newcomers receive their first snarky message from another editor or after their work is flagged, marked for deletion, or even worse, deleted altogether. These experiences can discourage those that may already be hesitant about sharing their writing work in a public forum (even if that forum is within a class – never mind the Internet itself) and more often than not, once one article or edit receives negative feedback or is marked for deletion, it invites other editors to negatively critique others working in the same space (often classes or edit-a-thons are tagged and organized). That is not to say that newcomers' work is always perfectly polished and ready for publication on Wikipedia's Mainspace (it often is riddled with issues indicative of a new learner), but then again Wikipedia's pages are always a work in progress. Furthermore, from a pedagogical standpoint (both in and out of the classroom) there is huge value to "learning in public" and learners are quick to make modifications from direct, constructive feedback. However, vague or curt commentary (biting) can often leave newcomers feeling deflated, not only limiting further participation but negating all the potential benefits from writing in a public space.

Some gatekeeping measures are explicit (discouraging new contributors, content-specific guidelines/conventions that are hard to find or decode) while others are a bit more subtle – challenging the "notability" of topics and biographical figures that editors deem inappropriate for inclusion. Of course, many of these examples (of gatekeeping) mirror various biases in practice offline, and reflect (often unconscious) cognitive biases of those enacting these practices. What is important to note in these examples is that these experiences are part of a larger system of community policing that remains hostile toward outsiders – one that is not necessarily easy to fix.

In our work as educators, we are well-aware of the issue of gatekeeping as something that will either deter or discourage a novice student editor. In fact, we often find ourselves in the position of recommending students work on content that is less-developed or rated lower on Wikipedia's assessment scale in order to help them avoid any negative feedback or potential edit reverts. This type of avoidance of highly trafficked and well-watched Wikipedia articles means that students end up working on less notable articles that are in need of development. This second attribute can certainly be beneficial for novice editors learning how and what to contribute to an article. At the same time, articles that have received less attention from editors, and that are less notable, are often those that are more difficult to edit – simply because there aren't as many secondary sources on the topic to build from. In our previous writing, we have described this as a kind of Catch-22 specific to both Wikipedia-based education. Students and teachers are often motivated to improve coverage of marginalized topics in Wikipedia,[5] but face difficulty when trying to locate sources, because those same topics are also marginalized in the broader culture. When steering students away from more mainstream topics, do educators teaching a Wikipedia-based assignment actually reinforce gatekeeping practices? While we attempt to bring the novice student editor into Wikipedia editing in a way that will result in a positive learning experience, we also inadvertently bar them from editing certain content in the encyclopedia, further complicating Wikipedia's promise of equitable participation.

Overt Harassment

In 2015, Wikimedia's Support and Safety team published the results of a harassment study that surveyed 3,845 Wikimedia users. While the Wikimedia community is obviously broader than English Wikipedia, their results provide a backdrop to more recent research. The survey found that "38% of the respondents could confidently recognise that they had been harassed…and 51% witnessed others being harassed."[6] The survey also identifies the following forms of harassment, ordered from most to least frequently reported: content/vandalism, trolling/flaming, name calling, discrimination, stalking, threats of violence, outing/doxing, impersonation, hacking, and revenge porn.[7] Racially charged, misogynistic, transphobic, homophobic, and other identity-based types of harassment are, unfortunately, too common in the Wikimedia community.

While the research conducted by Wikimedia examined forms of harassment experienced by all members of the Wikimedia community, research on Wikipedia's gender gap and the ways in which this gap has emerged and persists has informed our understandings of the treatment of women, trans, and non-binary participant identities in Wikipedia.[8] It has also led to additional scholarship on participation exclusion in the community, and more specifically the harassment of women and trans-identified editors. A more recent interview-based study of 25 women editors in Wikipedia suggested that for women attempting to navigate the encyclopedia's community, Wikipedia represents "a spectrum of safe and unsafe spaces" – with multiple types of harassment, stocking, and other issues reported frequently by participants.

Covering different online harassment experienced by women Wikipedia editors, the study exemplifies a variety of ways in which non-white, non-male editors have been harassed both on and off-Wiki. Participants noted that it was often the case that they (women) were subjected to repeated romantic advances by other (male) editors,

Participants discussed being stalked, both at in-person events and on-Wiki, to the extent that they were compelled to modify their interactions with the community. Additionally, participants reflected on experiences that they felt they were unable to edit particular content for fear of conflict or retribution from male editors (in the form of edit reverts, challenges to their contributions, or other types of questioning). Some participants even reported being verbally harassed with sexually charged name-calling, slurs, or pejorative and gendered epithets.[9] Unfortunately not only are these stories are all-too common amongst non-white or non-male editors, but these stories represent only the tip of a larger iceberg as these experiences were of those that continued to edit (and then tell their stories), rather than (as often is the case) ceasing participation in the community.

In addition to outlining the ways in which the participants have experienced harassment, the authors share three broader findings related to navigating the encyclopedia and its community. First, they insist the complex make-up of Wikipedia as an ecology of digital media spaces and that instead of "a single website" it is instead "a large dynamic territory with distinguishable yet porous subspaces, each of which cultivates cultures that influence the cultures of adjoining spaces and may even provide a problematic template for how these cultures should all operate."[10] What is helpful here to take from this is that when we speak of Wikipedia, and particularly the community of Wikipedia, it is a vast space with numerous projects, roles, and differing pieces that work both separately but also influence each other – there is no separating the "toxic" aspects and elements as each of the spaces infect each other. Remembering that these are active, enthusiastic volunteers who passionately donate their time to improve the encyclopedia underscores this finding as these are the volunteers *that persisted* through their negative experiences and, unlike many others, refused to leave the space they were told in many ways that they were unwelcome in.

Second, understanding the encyclopedia as a territory enabled interviewees to discuss how certain spaces within that territory may be safer than others, and also allows them to share suggestions on how Wikipedia and Wikimedia can work to create a safer environment, especially by "addressing bad behaviors" and "creating women-only spaces." While this first suggestion is being addressed in the creation of the Universal Code of Conduct, or UCoC (which we discuss further in this chapter as well as in Chapter 5) the suggestion to work toward "women-only spaces" has not, as of yet, been taken up by the Wikipedia community, and is yet to be considered. When volunteers for the "encyclopedia anyone can edit" turn to discuss how to create separate spaces just so they can continue to volunteer and do the work they want (for free), this is a troubling sign.

In the final finding of Menking et al.'s study, participants share strategies for "constructing safety for oneself." While this particular finding is potentially problematic in the sense that victims of harassment seem to be held responsible for managing their own safety, (rather than an approach that holds the community at large responsible) the strategies provided by women editors in Wikipedia illuminate the ways in which certain editors respond to issues of safety and try to assist other novice editors negotiate the community. "To construct safety for themselves," write Menking et al., "our interviewees engage in boundary work (e.g., identifying work they will and will not do) and emotion work (e.g., adapting their outward expressions of emotions)."[11]

It is important to point out here that these same editors facing forms of harassment in Wikipedia, women, trans, and non-binary individuals, as well as people of color are, in many of these examples and otherwise, taking on additional labor as a result of (or due to seeing others experience) harassment in one shape or another. Given the fact that Wikipedia already depends on voluntary labor that, for most contributors, must be completed in addition to job, family, and other obligations, such extra labor exacerbates the challenges already facing marginalized potential editors. Finding and carving out additional and new spaces, boundary work, and identity work are all extra efforts, emotional labor, and hoops to jump through just *to give their time away for free.*

Boundary work, for these participants, means avoiding editing certain pages that might be more closely monitored by other editors known to harass or troll any new contributors, for instance. But boundary work may also mean actively choosing certain offline activities to engage (or not). Such strategies, Menking et al. remind us, allow women "to avoid spaces they perceive as stressful and/or threatening – even when the community might benefit from their expertise – and to manage their participation in ways that decrease the potential for "drama" and conform to Wikipedia's norms."[12]

Additionally, participants noted that they felt compelled to police their emotions and way they expressed their identities, "particularly when it comes to avoiding the appearance of 'weakness'" or other unaccepted or marginalized attributes.[13] Veteran women editors, who have been effective in their long-term contributions to Wikipedia, have noted that they often take on alternate identities on Wikipedia, and work hard to manage their on-Wiki identity. Whether managing multiple accounts (technically a violation of policy) or just paying particular and extra attention to language in order to hide their identity, this creates extra work for editors trying to contribute.

Identity management is often a result or response to conflict events in which editors have already experienced harassment related to their identity. Such experiences can also lead to women editors being forced to negotiate what Menking and Erikson term "gendered 'feeling rules'" in Wikipedia. As one of their participants shares,

> [There was] one time that my sex was used against me in a way that did hurt me. I would appreciate it if you didn't [share the details] because I don't like to show weakness. We have a term for that on Wikipedia. We call it beans.[14,15]

The emotional labor involved in this and other scenarios shared by women editors is taken up after a specific conflict or harassment event. These women are forced to confront certain "feeling rules" that prevent them from actively speaking out or speaking back against certain harassment because they fear that doing so will result in the same behavior.

Extra labor, particularly emotional and identity management work, as a facet of marginalized editors' experiences in Wikipedia, cannot be separated from issues related to harassment, gatekeeping and other exclusionary functions of the Wikipedia community. Considering how this phenomenon adds additional barriers to contribute to what is supposedly an open community that "anyone can edit," it is also illustrative of our larger concern in this chapter. The assumption of equality in Wikipedia actively obscures its failures to promote equity. While the encyclopedia boasts an "open access" ethic, it assumes equality in its consideration of "access" and often can turn a blind eye to the (often invisible) struggles that those who do not feel actively included can experience, leaving the "equality" of the access inequitable at best, and at times toxic and exclusionary when so many editors face harassment and additional barriers to contribute.

Passive vs. Active Inclusion

We need to rethink the ways in which we understand Wikipedia's foundational principles to understand how they play a fundamental role in the exclusionary and inequitable experiences of many editors. Rather than assuming a passive assumption of equality and access, the lived experiences of editors point to the need for an active rather than passive inclusionary ethic. Exploring some of the ways to interrogate these principles helps to illuminate not only how the principles play a role in these issues, but how rethinking them can help to alleviate some of the larger issues within the community.

Starting from "Wikipedia's 5 Pillars" (covered in Chapter 1), Amanda Menking and Jon Rosenberg point out the need for fundamental changes to Wikipedia by interrogating and rewriting the pillars.[16] They posit that the pillars "contribute to the implicit values further excluding women and other marginalized peoples from participating in Wikipedia."[17] Noting here the "implicit" values within the pillars helps to frame the space in which Wikipedia has lacked in its inclusionary ethic – the principles, particularly the pillars, make implicit assumptions about the participants which *creates the space* for exclusion. Menking and Rosenberg turn toward these pillars to rewrite and re-imagine them with a more inclusive (feminist) epistemology, which can help to frame some better ways to think about the community. In particular, their revised third pillar states that "The Integrity of Wikipedia Is a Function of the Size and Breadth of Its Community."[18] This conceptual pillar acknowledges that the community itself is the foundation on which Wikipedia rests, and when that community is lacking in diversity, then the integrity of the project also suffers. As we have argued throughout this book, for Wikipedia to remain successful in its aim to represent diversity in both content and participation, the community needs to expand its representation and inclusion. Perhaps more importantly, and in order to work toward active inclusion, the Wikipedia community itself needs to both recognize and account for the multiple complex ways exclusion has been "baked in" to Wikipedia's epistemological structure from the very beginning.

In distinguishing between passive and active inclusion in the Wikipedia community, we first want to note that rather than judging different approaches we are instead observing and acknowledging that Wikipedia itself has always been passively inclusive toward potential participants with an assumption of equality instead of actively including and creating spaces for equity. This is not necessarily bad, but it creates an open door policy without fully realizing the inequitable situations to approach that door, enter the door, or exist comfortably once inside. We also want to note that there is a difference between types of inclusive behavior here when it comes to the community rather than content – numerous groups are doing excellent work on diversifying content (which is wonderful) but still working within the system and its formal and overt "rules" or policies without interrogating the actual issue of the community demographic, or working to diversify and expand the community. There is nothing *wrong* with these groups, and they are doing fantastic work – often their content diversification work contributes to a more welcoming (and therefore more inclusive) space for Wikipedia. All of these efforts are important to the larger project of collecting and distributing "the sum of all human knowledge." However, when discussing the community itself (as we are focusing on here), we see that more actively inclusionary practices are key to ensuring a more diverse user group as the integrity of Wikipedia remains reliant on the diversity of its community.[19]

A few examples of more actively inclusive practices are groups like *Black Lunch Table* and *AfroCrowd*, both which center black voices to discuss matters about Wikipedia (and elsewhere) and target inclusion of black voices as well as seeking to diversify content on black artists, and the *Wiki Education Foundation*, which recruits teachers to bring Wikipedia projects into the classroom. While it is apparent how groups like *Black Lunch Table* and *AfroCrowd* are actively inclusive in their outreach and programs, Wiki Education is also a prime example of active inclusion as it helps to diversify editors through educators that bring Wikipedia assignments into the classroom. These educators then guide students (often far more diverse than the demographics of Wikipedia) through the process, ensuring that they have a "safe space" (a guided and open space for discussion) to navigate, understand, and even critique both the community and the space of Wikipedia. These groups and their practices, as well as many like them, are actively creating spaces for new editors to learn and feel supported both on and off Wikipedia. These groups' continued success underscores the necessity of actively inclusive practices at a fundamental and base level on Wikipedia in order to effectively grow and diversify the editorship.

This all being said, the community at large definitely recognizes the need for change, and also recognizes the difficulty and complexity of this task in such a space. Emerging from the "Wikimedia 2030" discussions at Wikimania in Montreal 2017, and continued throughout the following years in numerous spaces, the community and the Wikimedia foundation outlined and drafted what is now known as the "Universal Code of Conduct" (UCoC). Discussed further in the next chapter, the UCoC makes explicit what was often only tangentially implicit (and then therefore interpreted in different ways, allowing for the aforementioned "power plays" and permissive of harassing behavior). This keys in on beginning to understand how this all went awry – passive inclusion and implicit assumptions baked into Wikipedia's principles are representative of how the space was not designed with equity in mind.

Inclusion Concerns at Its Core

As we have mentioned previously in this book, we offer criticism of Wikipedia in order to forward an honest and constructive perspective. While we admire the project for what it has accomplished, we also know that Wikipedia can make important strides to improve, especially in terms of social equity within the community. Having said that, it's equally important to acknowledge that many of Wikipedia's issues related to social exclusion are "baked-in" to the project's overarching ideology and culture, and have been from its start. Our discussion below attempts to excavate and uncover these broader ideological concerns, not for the purpose of casting blame on the community, its founders, or the project writ large, but for the purpose of providing a deep exploration of how these problems came about. In particular, we explore Wikipedia's homogenous culture-of-use, originating within a fairly narrow group of white, male, and well-educated community, as well as how certain norms in the encyclopedia demonstrate the overarching ideological positions this community forwarded in the encyclopedia's early days. These norms, formally known as guidelines in Wikipedia, reify an ethic of equality that obfuscates the encyclopedia's social problems, while also preventing the community's ability to achieve social equity.

Homogenous Culture-of-Use

In Chapter 1, we discussed Steven Thorne's concept "culture-of-use" to help explain the gap, or disconnect, between the explicit policies, guidelines, and other "official" rules in Wikipedia, and the actual practices that characterize the community – what is actually implemented. Using this as a framework for understanding the "historically sedimented associations, purposes, and values that accrue to a digital communication tool from its everyday use,"[20] we can better understand the foundations of Wikipedia and how the encyclopedia's pillars, policies, and guidelines emerged from assumptions about the users, creating a space for *those* assumed users. Early policies emerged from a male demographic, and the ways in which they have been engaged and enforced have, whether overtly or as a (unquestioned and unexamined) function of the foundational policies, been disempowering to underrepresented groups.

This is not to say that Wikipedia was formed with malicious intentions of exclusion, but instead to point out that, much like it is necessary for the integrity of the encyclopedia to diversify its editorship, a homogenous user base often lacks the perspective or consideration to be radically inclusive for those outside their own demographic. In short, Wikipedia's failure at diversity is because it never had diversity to begin with, as those who formulated its founding principles and policies did not conceptualize or understand what it took to be actively inclusive of a diverse editorship. This might have been understandable in its early formation over 20 years ago, but the issues that continue to persist are symptomatic of these early assumptions, and must be addressed. In particular, there are two major tenets of the Wikipedia community that exemplify these assumptions and their failures to include a plethora of voices: "Be Bold" and "Assume Good Faith." Examining these will help to open a space for critiquing and engaging some of these early assumptive tenets in ways can be productive for re-imagining and re-capturing the dream of well-intentioned techno-utopian ideals.

Be Bold

In the preface to this book, we wrote briefly about Wikipedia's "Be Bold" directive, an early editing guideline that, in its current form, encourages would-be editors to put aside their doubts and "feel free to make improvements to Wikipedia in a fair and accurate manner."[21] Wikipedia, the guideline explains, can only develop successfully when everyone contributes and actively works to fix issues or errors. When writing about this guideline in the preface, we noted how, although we understand the overarching "spirit" of "Be Bold" – we cannot help but attend to its underlying ideological implications. The question of "who gets to be bold," particularly in the context of an encyclopedia that was founded by white, English-speaking males with advanced college degrees must be raised.[22] Who gets to be bold when the majority of the editor base is male? And finally, what happens when new editors whose identities do not match the dominant ones are continually met with harassment or gatekeeping efforts?

As an editing guideline, the "Be Bold" directive can be seen as encouraging and even necessary advice for new Wikipedia editors. However, as a social norm inscribed by early Wikipedia editors and founders, Sanger, in particular, the directive can and should also be read as intrinsically prohibitive. Newcomers to Wikipedia, particularly those with marginalized identities, may choose to be bold, and still have their edits questioned or reverted. They may choose to be bold and face multiple types of harassment. In short, as minorities in a predominantly male community, the extent of their boldness won't necessarily translate into fair and equitable treatment by other editors.

Newcomers who access the Wikipedia article for this editing guideline are also warned, in a way, about the fact that other editors "will edit what you write." "Do not take it personally!," the guideline continues. "They, like all of us, just wish to make Wikipedia as good an encyclopedia as it can possibly be."[23] Behind the kind warning, the underlying assumption here is that other editors will not make it personal (when in fact we know they have and will continue to do so). Also of note in this guideline is its intrinsic connection to another guideline, "Assume Good Faith." In fact, the instruction "Do not take it personally!" is linked to the article on "Assume Good Faith."[24]

Assume Good Faith

It seems odd to criticize the concept of "Assume Good Faith" as the proper application of this tenet remains a cornerstone of many communities and friendships. In theory, assuming good faith of everyone's actions leads to better conflict resolution, better conversations, and less confrontational behavior. Much like "Be Bold," we understand both the reasoning for and the necessity of both of these tenets when it comes to creating a space for collaborative writing amongst anonymous (or pseudonymous) editors – the user must both "make the edit" and also hopes that other editors will see this as a "good faith effort." While all of this remains important for the space of Wikipedia, we must also ask the question whether the application of "Assume Good Faith" is always made in "good faith" and whether that narrative helps to create a safer space for gatekeepers, harassers, and other toxic members of the community.

However, it is important to point out that both historically and currently the assumption that someone "acts in good faith" has always been a privileged position. It goes without saying that this tenet does not speak as well to historically disenfranchised groups as it does to the lion's share of Wikipedia's editor demographic (Western, white, and male), particularly when it comes to the ways in which that demographic has both historically and currently denied the very same assumption toward others outside of its demographic. It is not to say that "assuming good faith" is not a great idea, only to point out that, much like "Be Bold," the identification with this concept might not be as universal as the authors of this idea had originally conceived.

Furthermore, this assumption of good faith also raises the question: even if (given the numerous cognitive biases that plague a homogenous user base) users *believe* they are acting "in good faith," could these biases themselves be covered up by this tenet and act as a barrier to properly inquiring about editorial decision-making? Of course, the answers to these questions are both impossible and obvious: we can never know the actual intentions, but we can see that whether "in good faith" or not, editors often act badly toward others on Wikipedia – particularly non-white, non-male newcomers. These assumptions allow for gatekeeping and "power plays" as the harassing editors can hide behind policy, acting "in good faith," while applying policy unequally and in a way that categorically targets marginalized voices.

Cognitive biases, whether acknowledged or conscious or not, disrupt these assumptions both on and off-Wiki, as the reality of the situation is that dominant groups are the recipients of the benefit of the doubt (or assumption of good faith) while historically disenfranchised groups continue to lack the same consideration. In the end, the assumption of good faith is both kind and well-intentioned, but it remains a fairytale when it comes to the reality of marginalized groups as good faith is often only assumed by and for those in power.

Working on Inclusion with Wikipedia Community Initiatives

At its core, Wikipedia is a social community and has always been so, both on and off-Wiki. From the global "Wikimania" conference, held every year since 2005, to regional conferences such as Wikiconference North America, to local and topical edit-a-thons, to small get-togethers and community groups, "Wikimedians" often gather in person to discuss the project and socialize with other community members. Such gatherings are especially important to consider as the community attempts to move toward a more equitable model for participant belonging. As discussed briefly above, the broader community should look toward groups such as *Wiki Education*, *Black Lunch Table*, *AfroCrowd*, and others to better understand a type of active inclusion that both invites and sustains membership among a more diverse community. The efforts of these types of groups are significant because they recognize the major issues within the encyclopedia, while also underscoring how difficult it is to change the culture of such a complex system. Obviously, there is much work to be done, but the point we would like to highlight here echoes Menking and Rosenberg's revised Wikipedia Pillar, "The Integrity of Wikipedia Is a Function of the Size and Breadth of Its Community." Yes, content is important, but when considering that Wikipedia has always been and remains a community, it remains imperative to consider those who create that content. Working to "bridge the gap" and improve representation of marginalized knowledge is not only an incredibly worthy endeavor in and of itself, as well as one that is also often more motivating to novice editors. However, if we recognize that Wikipedia's full integrity, its sustainability and value as a project for knowledge equity, is inherently linked to its people, it pins the future of Wikipedia upon its ability to change in this way for the better.

This is why looking toward organizations that center people over content is so important. As mentioned above, one such organization that has dramatically increased the community's diversity is Wiki Education. An offshoot of a public policy initiative begun by the Wikimedia Foundation in 2010, Wiki Education is now a separate nonprofit dedicated to supporting academic engagement with Wikipedia-based educational assignments. In this role, Wiki Education provides training and support for post-secondary students and teachers across all disciplines to enable them to effectively contribute to the encyclopedia as part of a classroom assignment. In just short of a decade of operation, students enrolled in a Wiki Education project have made an enormous impact on the encyclopedia, adding over 76 million words to the free knowledge project.

Such contributions should be applauded, but what makes Wiki Education especially unique is its capacity to actively diversify the Wikipedia community by inviting students into that community. Demographics of institutions of higher education are automatically more diverse than Wikipedia's community. In fact, Wiki Education has discovered that among its student editors participating in the program, 68% of them identify as women.[25] Finally, because it emphasizes the education (and to an extent, assimilation) of new editors, Wiki Education further works to actually help novices enter into and become part of Wikipedia's community.

To be fair, the broader Wikimedia community not only acknowledges problems like harassment, but has also actively worked against them through initiatives such as the Wikimedia-funded harassment study and the more recently developed UCoC. Attending to these smaller organizations, such as Wiki Education, also demonstrates the overall perseverance and sustainability of Wikipedia. As veteran instructors with Wiki Education, we have long admired the project for its ability to actively engage with complex issues such as Wikipedia's gender gap, and homogenous editor demographic. Ultimately, it is organizations like these, who are devoted to building social communities of people first, and improving content second, that will carry Wikipedia into a sustainable future.

Obviously, there is much work to be done in this incredibly complex and interconnected puzzle. The ways in which Wikipedia continues to function are both reliant on its community as well as its community remains a function of the tenets of Wikipedia, all potentially shifting in conversation and influence. Untangling these pieces to treat them separately is ultimately impossible, and although we can tease parts out to magnify and interrogate, the ways in which Wikipedia continues to make decisions about how to collect and distribute all the world's knowledge (and ultimately stand as the encyclopedic representation of reality) are ultimately interrelated and codependent. In the final chapter we attempt to think through these different pieces and address the larger concern about "whose reality" Wikipedia represents and how to continue the project of gathering the "sum of all human knowledge."

Notes

1 "Wikipedia: What Wikipedia Is Not," *Wikipedia*, accessed July 15, 2020, https://en.wikipedia.org/w/index.php?title=Wikipedia:What_Wikipedia_is_not&oldid=967817887.
2 Michel Foucault, *The Archaeology of Knowledge & The Discourse on Language* (New York: Vintage, 1982), 216.
3 Leigh Gruwell, "Wikipedia's Politics of Exclusion: Gender, Epistemology, and Feminist Rhetorical (In)Action," *Computers and Composition* 37 (September 1, 2015): 117–131, https://doi.org/10.1016/j.compcom.2015.06.009; Amanda Menking and Ingrid Erickson, "The Heart Work of Wikipedia: Gendered, Emotional Labor in the World's Largest Online Encyclopedia," in *Proceedings of the 33rd Annual ACM Conference on Human Factors in Computing Systems*, Seoul, Republic of Korea (2015): 207–210, https://doi.org/10.1145/2702123.2702514; Amanda Menking, Ingrid Erickson, and Wanda Pratt, "People Who Can Take It: How Women Wikipedians Negotiate and Navigate Safety," in *Proceedings of the 2019 CHI Conference on Human Factors in Computing Systems*, Glasgow, Scotland, UK, (2019): 1–14, https://doi.org/10.1145/3290605.3300702.
4 Ibid., 1.
5 Jiawei Xing and Matthew Vetter, "Editing for Equity: Understanding Instructor Motivations for Integrating Cross-Disciplinary Wikipedia Assignments," *First Monday*, May 25, 2020, https://doi.org/10.5210/fm.v25i6.10575.
6 "Harassment Survey," *Wikimedia Foundation*, 2015, https://upload.wikimedia.org/wikipedia/commons/5/52/Harassment_Survey_2015_-_Results_Report.pdf
7 "Harassment Survey."
8 Benjamin Collier and Julia Bear, "Conflict, Criticism, or Confidence: An Empirical Examination of the Gender Gap in Wikipedia Contributions," in *Proceedings of the ACM 2012 Conference on Computer Supported Cooperative Work*, New York, NY, USA (2012): 383–392, https://doi.org/10.1145/2145204.2145265; Eduardo Graells-Garrido, Mounia

Lalmas, and Filippo Menczer, "First Women, Second Sex: Gender Bias in Wikipedia," in *Proceedings of the 26th ACM Conference on Hypertext & Social Media*, New York, NY, USA (2015): 165–174, https://doi.org/10.1145/2700171.2791036; Heather Ford and Judy Wajcman, "'Anyone Can Edit', Not Everyone Does: Wikipedia's Infrastructure and the Gender Gap," *Social Studies of Science* 47, no. 4 (August 1, 2017): 511–527, https://doi.org/10.1177/0306312717692172.

9 Menking et al., "People Who Can Take It."

10 Ibid., 6.

11 Ibid., 9.

12 Ibid.

13 Ibid.

14 Menking and Erickson, "The Heart Work of Wikipedia," 209.

15 By "beans," this editor is alluding to an essay writing in project namespace that discusses the idea that telling people not to do something may result in the opposite result. See, "Wikipedia: Don't Stuff Beans up Your Nose," Wikipedia, last modified December 20, 2020. https://en.wikipedia.org/w/index.php?title=Wikipedia:Don%27t_stuff_beans_up_your_nose&oldid=995268172.

16 Amanda Menking and Jon Rosenberg, "WP:NOT, WP:NPOV, and Other Stories Wikipedia Tells Us: A Feminist Critique of Wikipedia's Epistemology," *Science, Technology, & Human Values* (May 13, 2020), https://doi.org/10.1177/0162243920924783.

17 Ibid., 9–10.

18 Ibid., 17.

19 Menking and Rosenberg.

20 Steven L. Thorne, "Cultures-of-Use and Morphologies of Communicative Action," *Language Learning & Technology* 20, no. 2 (2016): 185, http://llt.msu.edu/issues/june 2016/thorne.pdf.

21 "Wikipedia: Be Bold," in *Wikipedia*, last modified October 21, 2020. https://en.wikipedia.org/w/index.php?title=Wikipedia:Be_bold&oldid=984736314.

22 Larry Sanger finished a doctorate in Philosophy from Ohio State University in 2000; Jimmy Wales began a PhD program in Finance at the University of Alabama at Auburn; and later transferred to Indiana University, though never completing the dissertation requirement.

23 "Wikipedia: Be Bold."

24 "Wikipedia: Assume Good Faith," *Wikipedia*, last modified 6 December 2020, https://en.wikipedia.org/w/index.php?title=Wikipedia:Assume_good_faith&oldid=985510496.

25 How Do Students Change Wikipedia?" *Wiki Education*, last modified May 31, 2016, https://wikiedu.org/changing/wikipedia/.

5 The Reality That Shapes Wikipedia

> The real political task in a society such as ours is to criticize the workings of institutions that appear to be both neutral and independent.
>
> —Michel Foucault, *The Chomsky-Foucault Debate*

This book has sought to present a nuanced exploration of the online encyclopedia Wikipedia through an analysis of how Wikipedia constructs reliability; its policies and procedures for inclusion of certain information, and how that information becomes knowledge; and finally, into how the community welcomes or excludes participation. Throughout the previous chapters, we have demonstrated how the encyclopedia, for better or worse, has come to arbitrate on what types of information deserve to be preserved and curated as knowledge, and how this knowledge, in turn, shapes our reality. Although Wikipedia exists in over 270 language versions, we have primarily focused on the English Wikipedia due in large part to its dominance in the global knowledge economy, as well as its impact on our primary audience. This being said, the issues and concerns we lay out are not limited to English, the English Wikipedia, or even Wikipedia itself, and may be of consideration to a variety of knowledge production systems.

The concerns illuminated in the previous chapters identify issues not only within Wikipedia policies themselves, but also beyond the stated rules, these "hidden" systems that influence the construction of Wikipedia. The policies themselves are not necessarily broken, but they were written by and within a particular culture-of-use that exemplified "historically sedimented characteristics"[1] related to its male demographic and techno-utopian ethic. Whether or not they are well intentioned is not the concern, it is that they were imagined, crafted, and employed with a limited understanding or even concern with a larger ethic of inclusion. The core values of Wikipedia, of free

DOI: 10.4324/9781003094081-5

knowledge collection and dissemination, "work" insofar as they struggle for something positive and incredible, but the issues in which some of policies and guidelines have played out are at least partially due to the limitations of those who envisioned it and persist because of a myopic view of knowledge production based in these techno-utopian ideals. The questions that arise regarding what counts as knowledge, what should be included, and who gets to contribute become more imperative to engage with as gaps are exposed and seemingly equitable systems are found lacking. The lofty goal of collecting and distributing the "sum of all human knowledge" remains infinitely difficult enough, but questions of "who has access to what" in regard to reading, writing, and distribution to this "free" knowledge system become ever more complicated when excavating how Wikipedia is *actually* constructed. This new landscape of inquiries into the workings of Wikipedia assists in clarifying the immensely opaque system that constitutes knowledge construction.

This being said, while we have presented numerous issues and critiques of the encyclopedia throughout this book, our overall stance is (with reservations) celebratory of this incredible space. Despite issues related to its gender gap, the inability to represent indigenous knowledge that operates beyond print-culture, and other systemic, epistemological, and cognitive biases, Wikipedia remains the best example and possible option (so far) for gathering and making available human knowledge. While the encyclopedia has set what might be an unachievable goal, to create "a world in which every single person on the planet is given free access to the sum of all human knowledge,"[2] imagining this goal has proven exceptionally inspiring to the thousands of volunteers that helped to create the most comprehensive and accurate encyclopedia to date. With over 6 million (and counting) unique articles, the English Wikipedia provides access to reliable reference knowledge for millions of users on a daily basis. Furthermore, as an encyclopedia open to new editors, Wikipedia provides unique opportunities for users to participate in the continued production of its article content, improving our access to knowledge and opening up the process of knowledge production (at least on the surface) to more individuals.

This incredible repository of knowledge answers millions of inquiries per day, inspiring countless reactions, interactions, and fueling limitless and unknowable responses from its readers. From the way it is written in such formalized "neutral" tone, to what is included and excluded from its collection, to the manner it is presented through its Wiki interface, and most definitely through the community that maintains and constructs it, Wikipedia is not only a representation of reality, but partakes itself in constructing "reality" for those touched by it – and with billions of pageviews a month, and millions upon millions of users, there are few left and little that remains untouched.

Through exploration of how Wikipedia functions as not only an encyclopedia but the de facto representation of reality as the largest repository of knowledge ever created, how it constructs facts and "truth" through reliability and verifiability, how it defines "what counts as knowledge" through notability and its related policies, and how its community shapes itself on and off-Wiki, we have teased out not only the policies and their implementation, but some of the ways in which Wikipedia is shaped through unwritten rules, unacknowledged forces, and hidden games. These explorations help to engage "better questions" in regard to how Wikipedia represents "the sum of all human knowledge" and how we might better engage and understand both the causes of the issues as well as the potential for change. In this final chapter we turn toward these questions, exploring and refining the critical areas of Wikipedia's unstated conditions and relations that weigh so heavily on its construction.

Moving beyond the policies and procedures, we examine the areas in which Wikipedia continues to struggle in its lofty goals. Through this examination and our understanding of its construction, we will offer up some engagements, recommendations, and hope for the future of Wikipedia.

The Realities of Reliability, Exclusion, and Community

Throughout the previous chapters we elucidated the manner in which Wikipedia shapes its content. As the largest repository of knowledge ever collected, Wikipedia remains both an astounding human achievement as well as endless opportunity for improvement, both in content and in community. From the construction of reliability, to the included (and excluded content), to the manner in which Wikipedia's community shapes itself (and therefore its policies), we have teased apart the inner-workings of Wikipedia in hopes to illuminate this complex system of knowledge representation. Wikipedia functions (for better or worse) to shape the information repository which in turn shapes our reality, and the exposition of these innerworkings allowed us to embark on a more rigorous critique of the encyclopedia and its constitutive elements. Exposing these areas for critique illustrates a variety of blind spots that, when seen together, help to further reveal opportunities to both understand the ways that Wikipedia shapes reality as well as help to bring its stated intentions and goals in line with the actuality of Wikipedia's construction. Through exposing these inner workings, the actuality of Wikipedia's constitution (and therefore shaping of reality) can be more plainly seen as to understand both the present situation as well as better light a path toward the future of the encyclopedia.

As we explained in Chapter 1, Wikipedia has no shortage of formal policies and guidelines governing the production of content and behavior in the encyclopedia. The official rules don't always adequately describe what actually occurs, however. In order to elucidate the hidden implementation of such rules, this book has argued for an archaeological approach to reveal the unspoken rules existing beneath the discursive practices of Wikipedia. Accordingly, our review of Wikipedia's 5 Pillars, for instance, not only explains each pillar on its own terms, it also uncovers something hidden about each pillar's invisible work. Wikipedia is "an encyclopedia" – it is also *the encyclopedia.* Its status as *the* de facto reference for global knowledge and wide-ranging usage ensures that Wikipedia shapes reality through its representations of the known world. Because Wikipedia is an encyclopedia, it also carries certain epistemological traits of that genre, and its curation of knowledge influences particular ways of knowing information and reality. Examining the remaining four pillars in this chapter also allows us to demonstrate Wikipedia's ongoing construction of reality through its insistence on neutrality, FLOSS ethic and ideology, guidelines for civil behavior, and finally, dedication to the idea that the encyclopedia can change ("No Firm Rules"). Ultimately, we demonstrate how Wikipedia operates as a cultural hegemony in that it both creates the conditions in which human knowledge is represented and serves as the (best possible option for the) representation of all human knowledge. From this starting point, it becomes evident not only why Wikipedia is so important to the representation of knowledge, and how modern society understands what constitutes reality itself, but that Wikipedia's system of knowledge construction is most often misunderstood and requires further exploration, which offers space for better (and necessary) critique.

Chapter 2 explores both the formal policies for evaluating and processing information and what happens beneath the surface as the encyclopedia community works to construct reliability. Continuing the concern from Chapter 1, we argue that Wikipedia's method of cultural hegemony is both epistemological and ontological. Wikipedia's hegemonic power is epistemological in the sense that Wikipedia assumes authority to distinguish between information and knowledge through the manner in which it assesses and constructs reliability. Not only does it make these important distinctions, but the encyclopedia creates the conditions and guidelines through which information *becomes* knowledge. Of special significance here is that many of those conditions and guidelines remain rooted in a logocentric conception of knowledge, which brings about its own concerns and issues. Exploring what goes on behind the scenes, how policies are implemented (whether equitably or not) by the community, also demonstrates how the encyclopedia provides a model of reliability that is both grounded in policy as well as distributed and social – what we term "ethical assemblages."

Attending to this model of ethical assemblages also enables our realization of Wikipedia's ontological ramifications, especially as it relates to users' information behaviors. Understanding the distributed and participatory construction of reliability within Wikipedia, we argue, opens up pathways for critical media literacy. As users become more comfortable in engaging in processes of evaluation that move beyond static conceptions of credibility (e.g., C.R.A.A.P.), they also begin to view credibility as a dynamic process rather than an isolated event.

Chapter 3's focus on Notability (WP:N) further describes Wikipedia's processes of cultural hegemony in that the policies, and enactments of those policies, determine what (and often "who") counts as knowledge. Our analysis of the Notability policy examines both the formally stated policies and guidelines, as well as the actual practices ensuing from those formal texts, which are very often impacted by cognitive and systemic biases, the availability (and accessibility) of secondary texts on particular topics. In this chapter, we argue that notability policies function in two distinct and often conflicting ways. First, the policy of Notability further serves Wikipedia's project for becoming a reliable source as it helps editors exclude articles on topics that do not warrant coverage. At the same time, policies surrounding Notability also act as gatekeeping devices that significantly limit representation of already marginalized topics and identities (see our discussions of Donna Strickland and Clarice Phelps, for example).

The community organizing functions of Wikipedia are further detailed in Chapter 4 as we explore Wikipedia community and engagement, and especially how the community determines who is enabled to contribute. Although Wikipedia is both known and advertised as the "free encyclopedia that anyone can edit," the actual community practices do not always match this utopian vision. In fact, the community has long struggled (and continues to struggle) with gatekeeping, harassment, outreach, and inclusion. This chapter has provided a fuller examination of these issues, paying special attention to Wikipedia's homogenous editorial demographic and how the foundational ideas, while utopian and inclusive on the surface, have served the assumptions of the homogenous culture of use and therefore exclude much-needed diversity in its editorship.

Of course, the community itself remains the key to understanding Wikipedia and the ways in which it constructs its depiction of reality. The policies, procedures, and guidelines remain written by, supported by, and enforced by the community. Furthermore, the ways in which the community encourages or discourages certain types of behavior, whether meaning to or not, remain a function of the community's self-policing. As with all policies, Wikipedia's policies are only as good as their enforcement, and, vibrant and justice-oriented community or not, the burden on a volunteer community to equitably enforce hundreds of policies remains, if nothing else, incredibly daunting.

Wikipedia Remains the Last Best Place on the Internet

In an age where misinformation continues to expand in both its scope and influence, the Wikipedia community has developed a comprehensive and fairly effective system for evaluating information to ensure reliability. As we have thoroughly discussed in Chapter 2, Wikipedia has also demonstrated a significant capability to combat misinformation, without which, it could not even begin to offer us a chance at knowledge equity.[3] As Alex Pasternack recognizes,

> while places like Facebook, YouTube, and Twitter struggle to fend off a barrage of false content, with their scattershot mix of policies, fact-checkers, and algorithms, one of the web's most robust weapons against misinformation is an archaic-looking website written by anyone with an internet connection, and moderated by a largely anonymous crew of volunteers.[4]

Indeed, Wikipedia effectively dodged criticism related to misinformation and fake news that plagued other social media sites strictly because its entire existence is motivated by its mission to "battle fake news." Pete Forsyth, a long-time editor and key architect in Wikipedia's public policy initiative (which later led to Wiki Education), further describes this mission by contrasting the encyclopedia community with other social media platforms:

> Wikipedia's fundamental purpose is to present facts, verified by respected sources. That's different from social media platforms, which have a more complex project...they need to maximize engagement, and get people to give up personal information and spend money with advertisers. Wikipedia's core purpose involves

> battling things like propaganda and 'fake news.' Other platforms are finding they need to retrofit their products to address misinformation; but battling fake news has been a central principle of Wikipedia since the early days.[5]

This "battle" with fake news can also be seen in how the encyclopedia addresses current political events and its associated articles. Take the 2020 U.S. Presidential Election, for example. By October 21, 2020, articles on "Donald Trump," "Joe Biden," "Kamala Harris" and the "2020 United States presidential election" had all been locked down, open only to editors with "extended confirmed protection" (accounts at least 30 days old and with at least 500 edits). Putting this lock in place, something which only an editor with administrative privileges can do, limits the ability of would-be vandals to spread misinformation during a critical time: the weeks leading up to November 6, 2020, as Americans cast their votes. In fact, as recognized by Sara Morrison in a feature appearing in the online magazine *Vox,* "How Wikipedia is Preparing for Election Day," the community engages in a lengthy discussion about how a winner should be declared (among other issues) weeks and even months before the event. "There's no rush to be the first to declare a winner," Morrison writes, "(quite the opposite in fact)."[6]

The encyclopedia's ability to ward off misinformation is largely due to its robust system of policies for evaluating information (discussed at length in Chapter 2). But it is also due to Wikipedia's status as a nonprofit organization. When compared to other social and participatory media, as Pasternack does above, Wikipedia is an exceptionally and altogether different creature. Compared to Facebook and Google, Wikipedia is a project in altruism – its data is created by its users, rather than farmed from them. It has no commercial incentive beyond sustaining the project, and no interest in capturing information about its users to sell to advertisers. As "the only privacy-respecting site among the top online sites,"[7] Wikipedia remains a relic of the old participatory and democratic web promised in the 1990s.

More to the point, Wikipedia exists outside of what economic theorist Shoshana Zuboff has termed surveillance capitalism, "A new economic order that claims human experience as free raw materials for hidden commercial practices of extraction, prediction, and sales."[8] Zuboff's theorization of surveillance capitalism explains the new market logic behind tech giants such as Google and Facebook, as she acknowledges a new set of relations surrounding product, customers, and value:

> Surveillance capitalism's products and services are not the objects of value exchange. They do not establish constructive

> producer-consumer reciprocities. Instead, they are the 'hooks' that lure users into their extractive operations in which our personal experiences are scraped and packaged as the means to others' ends. We are not surveillance capitalism's 'customers.' Although the saying tells us 'If it's free, then you are the product," that is also incorrect. We are the sources of surveillance capitalism's crucial surplus: the objects of a technologically advanced and increasingly inescapable raw-material-extraction operation. Surveillance capitalism's actual customers are the enterprises that trade in its markets for future behavior.[9]

Zuboff further contrasts "surveillance capitalism" with the older order of the web, acknowledging how the former has "betrayed the hopes and expectations of many 'netizens' who cherished the emancipatory promise of the networked milieu."[10] This "emancipatory promise" is perhaps what continues to draw us to a community like Wikipedia. Its (techno)optimistic rhetoric, its encyclopedic ambitions, as we discussed in Chapter 1, offer a kind of promise that rarely exists on the contemporary web. As Robert Cooke notes, Wikipedia exists as "the last best place on the Internet…one of the few remaining places that retains the faintly utopian glow of early World Wide Web."[11]

Beyond this promise, however, Wikipedia offers an alternative to the "epistemic inequality" that characterizes so much of the contemporary digital world. Epistemic inequality "recalls a pre-Gutenberg era of extreme asymmetries of knowledge and the power that accrues to such knowledge."[12] Zuboff connects this term to surveillance capitalism by acknowledging how tech giants like Facebook and Google have "seize[d] control of information and learning itself":

> Epistemic inequality is not based on what we can earn but rather on what we can learn. It is defined as unequal access to learning imposed by private commercial mechanisms of information capture, production, analysis and sales. It is best exemplified in the fast-growing abyss between what we know and what is known about us….The new centrality of epistemic inequality signals a power shift from the ownership of the means of production, which defined the politics of the 20th century, to the ownership of the production of meaning. The challenges of epistemic justice and epistemic rights in this new era are summarized in three essential questions about knowledge, authority and power: Who knows? Who decides who knows? Who decides who decides who knows?[13]

Significantly, Zuboff makes no mention of Wikipedia (or its parent organization Wikimedia), one of the few communities on the web that is actually having legitimate conversations regarding "promoting knowledge equity," and has named such a project as a strategic goal.[14] In fact, in many ways, Wikimedia provides at least some answer to the three "essential questions" posed by Zuboff, as it further describes a dedication to knowledge equity in the following: "Our mission is to **set knowledge free**. We work to ensure that **everyone**, **everywhere** has equitable access to *create and consume information*."[15] Wikipedia's community works tirelessly to address Zuboff's questions in its mission. While we have demonstrated (among other things) that this particular mission has not yet been fully realized, it remains crucially important to acknowledge that the encyclopedia offers an alternative to the status quo of epistemic inequality. It is a remnant of Web 2.0 that continues to operate under the premise (and promise) of equity on the web. Despite its homogenous editorial demographic, Wikipedia also allows more opportunities for casual users to share in the production and consumption of knowledge than any other contemporary social media.

Furthermore, it can be argued that Wikipedia's success is at least partially due to its non-profit status. As Yochai Benkler notes,

> [Wikipedia's] resistance to market incentives has played a critical role in its adherence to a reasonable conception of truth as resulting from honest engagement by a community of practice, implemented as a facility that does not seek to manipulate and control its readers.

Like Zuboff, Benkler is also concerned with surveillance capitalism's threat to "use massive amounts of data they collect on each of us to shape both commercial demand and political outcomes." In the context of such a threat, Wikipedia remains an alternative to neoliberalism in that it has "justified the idea that having a significant source of knowledge that is free of markets and marches to the beat of a different drum having nothing to do with dollars is of critical importance."[16] We must acknowledge this importance as a significant aspect of Wikipedia's free(dom).[17] The encyclopedia's continued success, in many ways, will also determine the future of FLOSS projects and digital communities that are not functioning as surveillance capitalism engines primarily motivated by financial exigencies. However, to best ensure success and continued sustainability, the community will need to face some hard challenges, especially related to representation.

Mending Wikipedia's Representation Problems

Despite its numerous successes, Wikipedia remains plagued with numerous problems, particularly issues around representation, both in terms of participation and content. However, Wikipedia recognizes this, and, as mentioned above, Wikimedia seems committed to what the community calls "knowledge equity," so much so that it has identified this as a goal in its 2030 strategic plan:[18]

> As a social movement we will focus our efforts on the knowledge and communities that have been left out by structures of power and privilege. We will welcome people from every background to build strong and diverse communities. We will break down the social, political, and technical barriers preventing people from accessing and contributing to free knowledge.[19]

While we applaud the vision represented in this particular strategic goal, we also realize the complexity of the task. As we have shown throughout, many of the policies that ensure accuracy and reliability in the encyclopedia also create barriers to representation. Wikipedia's insistence on print verifiability, while it serves an important role in validating reliability of sources, also prevents the encyclopedia from representing knowledge "left out by structures of power and privilege."[20] Furthermore, while much work remains to be done in terms of encouraging more diverse participation beyond the encyclopedia's homogenous editorial demographic, many would-be editors still find the encyclopedia to be unwelcoming, or worse, hostile.

The encyclopedia is powered by volunteer labor, which is itself difficult to manage, but more so when the volunteer labor has contributed to the larger systemic representation issues. While WikiProjects such as Women in Red and other initiatives have encouraged editors to work on content gaps related to marginalized topics and issues, it is difficult to assimilate new editors, and onerous to encourage existing editors to work on topics that they are not intrinsically motivated by.

Of course, Wikipedia remains plagued by gatekeeping and harassing editors. These editors often block new content using existing policy rationales, are not invested in global or multicultural representation, and resist critiques of Wikipedia's investment in Eurocentric rationalism. Such gatekeepers often exclude content and contributors through the use of "power plays" that employ broad and often ambiguous Wikipedia policies as rationales for reverts and other editorial actions (most often deletionist in nature).[21]

In the concluding pages we offer some hope for Wikipedia by addressing some of the areas of concern with current and future plans for community improvement, as well as some suggestions for re-thinking how we can preserve, improve, and care for this incredible treasure of knowledge so that it can continue its journey to provide access to the sum of all human knowledge.

As Wikipedia continues to "represent" reality, it remains imperative to address and critique issues of representation in Wikipedia as they influence the "reality" Wikipedia attempts to represent. Although not exhaustive, the issues that remain of concern for Wikipedia fall roughly into five (often overlapping) areas:

1 Homogeneity of the editorial demographic, the continued lack of diversity within the ranks of English Wikipedia editors
2 Gaps in representation, the (visible and invisible) content gaps associated with the editorial demographic, societal and/or media marginalization, or other causes
3 Epistemological narrowness, the refusal to look beyond print-centric, and Western conceptions of knowledge-making to work with alternative traditions (e.g., oral and other folk or indigenous epistemologies)
4 The difficulty of managing volunteer labor, especially in regard to encouraging volunteer editors to work on marginalized content
5 Gatekeeping impulses and harassing behavior, especially a culture of using Wikipedia policy to block new content and discourage new editors

Wikimedia's strategic direction for 2030, first articulated in 2017, states that "By 2030, Wikimedia will become the essential infrastructure of the ecosystem of free knowledge, and anyone who shares our vision will be able to join us."[22] The principal foci of the strategic direction include: knowledge as service, or ensuring free access across communities and infrastructures to open knowledge; and, knowledge equity, ensuring engagement with issues of knowledge, privilege, and marginalization.

In terms of executing the strategic direction, among other actions, Wikimedia initiated the drafting of a new document, the Universal Code of Conduct, or UCoC. Wikimedia describes the process in the following:

> The Universal Code of Conduct (UCoC) is one of the key policy initiatives that has come out of the Wikimedia 2030 community

> conversations and strategy process. Wikimedians from around the world have put forth 10 recommendations to guide the movement towards its 2030 vision. One of these recommendations, to "Provide for Safety and Inclusion," included creating a Code of Conduct, the UCoC. It aims to provide a universal baseline of acceptable behavior for the entire movement without tolerance for harassment. The UCoC is being developed in consultation with the Wikimedia community with respect to context, existing local policies, as well as enforcement and conflict resolution structures.[23]

It should be noted that, as of the time of writing, these particular recommendations have only recently completed the first phase of "community and stakeholder dialogue." The second phase, which will "focus on how to enforce the UCoC," has yet to be completed.[24] However, these recommendations (summarized below) represent a major step in recognizing and addressing some of the major challenges Wikipedia faces going forward. It should be noted that, while UCoC is indicative of how the community has attempted to address certain challenges; the initiative is not, however, a panacea to Wikipedia's problems.

In its current draft form, the UCoC includes four major sections: a rationale, "Why we have a Universal Code of Conduct,' an introduction, a section on "Expected behaviour" and one on "Unacceptable behavior."[25] As becomes evident in its rationale and introduction, the UCoC is meant to address a number of challenges Wikipedia faces, (and that we have listed above). Among these, the UCoC seeks to "empower as many people as possible to actively participate in Wikimedia projects and spaces, to reach our vision of a world in which everyone can share in the sum of all human knowledge."[26]

Such a goal would, at least on the surface, work toward addressing editorial demographic homogeneity and content gaps, as it seeks to create a more welcoming community, and thus allow for more diversity of editors. The UCoC, furthermore, articulates that this empowering and inclusive environment can be accomplished by providing a "baseline of behavior for collaboration on Wikimedia projects worldwide," including, of course, the English Wikipedia. Among the "expected" behaviors, the document lists "mutual respect" which serves as a section heading for the following behaviors: "Practice empathy," "Assume Good Faith, and engage in constructive edits," and "Respect the way that contributors name and describe themselves." This section also includes the heading "Civility, collegiality, mutual support and good citizenship, which further includes the behaviors of "Mentorship and coaching," "Looking out for fellow contributors," and "Recognize and credit the work done by contributors."

For "Unacceptable behaviors,' the document lists "Harassment" (including "Insults," "Sexual Harassment," "Threats," "Encouraging harm to others," "Disclosure of personal data (Doxing)," "Hounding," and "Trolling." A subsection on "Abuse of power, privilege, or influence" and "Content vandalism and abuse of the projects" follows.

Expectations for behavior are not completely new in Wikipedia. In fact, "Assume Good Faith" (WP:AGF), a behavioral guideline that asks Wikipedians to respect the editorial actions of other users, has been around since at least 2004.[27] The fourth pillar of the encyclopedia asks editors to "treat each other with respect and civility."[28] Rather, what's new here is (1) the application of this code of conduct across all Wikimedia projects, and (2) the level of specificity meant to directly respond to issues related to the larger strategic goals of knowledge as service and knowledge equity. In issuing this particular code of conduct for expected and unacceptable behavior, Wikipedia also acknowledges problems related to the editor demographic, content gaps, and gatekeeping impulses of existing editors. If the community can find a way to enforce the new codes, we may expect to see some change around these particular issues. In terms of the other challenges we identified, it may be more difficult for the community to address the encyclopedia's epistemological narrowness and management of volunteer labor. UCoC represents an important step, but still a partial solution to these many challenges, as well as an indication of specific measures that can be taken to effectively meet these challenges.

Limiting Gatekeeping and Gatekeeper Influence

Wikipedia is based on a principle that already requires a significant sense of agency and confidence to participate. To "Be Bold" assumes a type of confidence and agency to edit, and remains a fundamental principle of Wikipedia, and really a cornerstone of collaborative knowledge production in general. This assumption comes with its own concerns and issues, as many users lack this confidence and agency to participate in such a manner. This is not to say that this is something that could fundamentally change – even with workshops and training, to contribute to Wikipedia, one must still "make the change" happen themselves. However, it is important to acknowledge that even before the policies, rules, technical skills, and other knowledge that must be understood to edit Wikipedia, the first step for many is simply knowing that they are *welcome* to participate, which underscores the absolute necessity to ensure a positive community experience, especially for new editors. The experience of a new editor in Wikipedia is difficult enough, but when "the encyclopedia anyone can edit" is marred by deletionists utilizing their specialized knowledge to gatekeep and exclude contributions, the community itself becomes an insurmountable obstacle to participation.

Throughout this book, we have illustrated how Wikipedia employs a strong bureaucratic system, utilizing a hierarchical system of user levels to function effectively. This bureaucratic system both helps the community function relatively cohesively as well as (for better or worse) creates barriers for participation in this complex system. Of course, in any collaborative system there must exist some manner of barrier for full access – even if everyone has the best intentions, new users must learn how to navigate the space. However, when the complex bureaucratic system requires extensive knowledge of potentially vague policies, it allows for a small minority of users to control content with little recourse or ability for most to participate. As we discuss more thoroughly in Chapter 3, gatekeeping impulses are often carried out by editors with high-level user status and thorough knowledge of Wikipedia. Such gatekeeping becomes successful through editors' "power plays" that engage specific policy rationales for removing or deleting content created by new and/or inexperienced editors. Furthermore, hiding behind policy and guidelines, these users can influence decision-making to exclude marginalized voices.

The success of gatekeepers points to a larger issue in Wikipedia: the extensive knowledge required to effectively participate in the encyclopedia's ongoing production. Wikipedia calls itself the online encyclopedia that anyone can edit. And in theory, this remains relatively accurate. However, when a novice's contribution is immediately reverted, or a new biographical article on a marginalized figure is immediately nominated for deletion, we must not only question the motives behind these particular actions, but also recognize this as a manner in which users are told that they are not welcome to participate. Policy rationales used to argue for particular reverts or deletion nominations are part of an expert editor's deep understanding of what has become a very complex system which sets them apart from the majority of editors and provides them with substantial power to shape the encyclopedia and the perception of the community to new users.

To participate fully and equitably in the encyclopedia and to gain agency and power in that system requires a substantial amount of technical, procedural, and legalistic knowledge. Technical knowledge, or an understanding of basic functions, wiki syntax, and editorial interface allows a user to actually make an edit. But this is only the beginning to a functioning and effective participation. Users must also gain a procedural understanding of processes related to article assessment, patrolling, and other aspects of evaluation. Finally, users must also understand the often very legalistic policies associated with notability, as discussed in Chapter 3, and Neutral Point of View, as discussed in Chapter 2. Without this knowledge, their contributions may be unlikely to persist, signaling that they are unwelcome. Furthermore, participation in any disagreement or decision-making process on Wikipedia requires not only all of this specialized knowledge but also an incredible amount of time, a privilege many do not have. To shift this balance of power and create a more welcoming community, Wikipedia must rethink some of its ways that it allows gatekeeping and undue influence.

One way that Wikipedia has already begun to work on becoming more welcoming and inclusive is deployment of the UCoC, which can be employed in a stronger way to reduce the power of those who are seeking to undermine the community. The community must acknowledge, however, that the UCoC cannot necessarily address the major challenges facing Wikipedia, especially the issue of gatekeeping. While the gatekeeping problem isn't easily solved, the UCoC, which gives the community a more codified set of guidelines to call out bad behavior, represents an important beginning.

Though it may be optimistic, we also see engagements such as this, and others like it, as part of the solution. By engaging in thorough and nuanced explorations of key policies and procedures in Wikipedia, both in terms of their visible and invisible manifestations, we have sought to create a resource for everyday users who wish to better understand how Wikipedia works and navigate its often troubled waters. Education initiatives such as the Wiki Education foundation and Wikimedia Education group can also play an important role in this, as they engage students in both how the encyclopedia works epistemologically as well as how to engage with it. While much of the early academic criticism and suspicion regarding the encyclopedia has waned, educational organizations and institutions still have much to learn. As Wikipedia shapes the representation of reality, educators have an important role to play both by participating in shaping knowledge production while also teaching ever-important information literacy skills gained from teaching with Wikipedia.[29]

Stronger Commitment to Diverse Knowledge

With initiatives like the UCoC and Wikimedia foundation's investment in non-Western training and community projects, Wikipedia's future remains bright. In particular, the codification of UCoC signals an important step as well as an ongoing commitment to change, as it aims to create a more welcoming and inclusive community should encourage more diversity among participants. However, as is the case with much of our discussions throughout this book, policy itself is never the entire solution. Many of the problematic behaviors and aspects of the community already defy long standing community principles and guidelines. "Assume Good Faith" (first developed in 2004)[30] and "Please do not bite the newcomers"[31] (2003) are two examples of formal rules that attempted to alleviate many of the same issues the UCoC addresses. However, as we previously pointed out, many of these formalized rules have been more implicit than explicit, and continued to allow the space for bad behavior. Successfully building and encouraging a diverse and robust community and including marginalized voices will need to more deeply engage not only community behavior but also how policies such as Verifiability and NPOV have limited the inclusion of alternative knowledge traditions.[32] Such consideration should include: (1) broad-based community input from stakeholders within and beyond the immediate community; (2) deep reflection on Wikipedia's place in the tradition of encyclopedic genre (itself a fairly Western textual construct); (3) an outcome-oriented structure for policy recommendations; (4) a commitment to raising awareness regarding Wikipedia's knowledge-making affordances and constraints within educational and other public sectors. Throughout the book, we have stressed the importance of understanding Wikipedia as somewhat constrained by its encyclopedic function. This is not to say that Wikipedia must move away from its encyclopedic identity, but instead to engage and acknowledge the encyclopedic genre as inherently oppressive to certain knowledge systems beyond a Western content. Wikipedia has grown tremendously in terms of public trust and credibility in the last decade, and we believe that part of this growth is due to its admission of issues related to the gender gap; Admitting faults, along with more transparency, builds trust. Additional reflection and transparency around dominant epistemological traditions bolsters this trust and allows for better critique and engagement. In the end, Wikipedia's ability to change and evolve its policies to foster a strong, safe, and diverse community will ensure a better encyclopedia, but it is the ability to reflect upon itself and change that remains the key to Wikipedia's future of representing the world's knowledge.

Knowledge Production and Representation Requires Constant Revolution

In Chapter 2, we argue that one way to resolve Wikipedia's neglect of indigenous knowledge and knowledge-making practices is to view the encyclopedia as always in a state of flux. This state of flux applies both to mainspace content, which is constantly being added to, improved, and updated as needed, as well as to the many project pages that attempt to govern how Wikipedia functions. In making this argument, we invoke the encyclopedia's Fifth Pillar, "Wikipedia has no firm rules"[33] to show that Wikipedia's dynamism is perhaps one of its most important assets going forward. In order to continue its fight for knowledge as service and knowledge equity, Wikipedia requires constant revolution. Such revolution does not mean upheaval, but a continual affirmation of some of its most original principles that enabled the community to be proactive in the development of new ways of handling specific challenges. When, not if, the encyclopedia becomes more diverse in terms of its editorial demographic, that demographic should also feel empowered to modify the "rules" to best suit their needs and to meet the challenges of building knowledge in an increasingly volatile world.

Wikipedia's Greatest Potential Is Change

In the end, Wikipedia remains one of the most incredible collections of knowledge ever created. Its longevity is a testament to the utopian dreams of early Internet pioneers, and one of the last remaining spaces where Web 2.0 persists in a manner unblemished by surveillance capitalism and the epistemic inequalities of the modern web. Wikipedia stands not only in stark contrast against these modern Internet issues, but can act as an antibody toward many of the concerns that emerged. Whether combatting disinformation or providing equitable knowledge access, Wikipedia continues to stand tall while other platforms struggle to balance their business models with implementing ethical approaches. Complex, frustrating, often messy, riddled with knowledge gaps, community failings, and a dwindling editor base, Wikipedia is not without issues of fault. However, as discussed throughout the previous chapters, the issue remains that, insofar as it is a community, *Wikipedia is human* and falls prey to human issues of bias, miscommunication, and negligence. However, despite its downsides, one of its greatest strengths of Wikipedia is exactly its greatest issue – the community continues to guide it, and Wikipedia can constantly change, grow, and evolve.

Wikipedia's ability to undergo constant evolution and change, despite its frustrating and messy process, remains its greatest strength and hope for the future. Throughout the previous chapters, we have explored numerous community concerns, many of which are actively discussed, dissected, and expounded upon both on and off-Wiki by Wikipedians worldwide. Addressing many of these issues remains a high priority for the foundation as well as the community, as evidenced by the continued focus on Wikipedia's future in the Wikipedia 2030 vision.

Wikipedia also affects change through the ways it represents reality. Its commitment to reliability, verifiability, and neutrality help to combat misinformation and disinformation in the largest and most accessed repository of knowledge in the world. What and how Wikipedia represents has influenced information has been verified across numerous platforms as its open licensing allows for it to be used in information verification to warn against misleading or incorrect information. Furthermore, engaging with Wikipedia as an editor has shown positive results for learning critical information literacy skills, shaping how people engage with the reality of our age of misinformation.[34] However, with only %0.05 of users editing Wikipedia, those actually engaging with Wikipedia is tragically low, and those who understand its inner-workings even lower. As we have discussed at length, Wikipedia's community is notoriously difficult to penetrate for new users, and for some, the first step of being "bold" and making the edit remains daunting enough to discourage participation at all.

In Chapter 4, we explored the gendered logic of one of Wikipedia's earliest guidelines, "Be Bold." Indeed, we are all socialized into a world that has already scripted boldness as a disposition belonging to a certain group of people – assumption of agency is not universal, and remains indicative of a certain type of privilege. This first barrier to participation precludes any other issue explored throughout this book, and all the concerns raised here are only amplified by the assumption of agency that Wikipedia demands to participate.

It is clear we need a new kind of boldness. One that is not merely an assumption of agency, but an active construction and inclusion. An invitation. Not only for Wikipedia, but for all knowledge production systems – it is not enough to be passively inclusive; but if Wikipedia is to remain entrusted with its grand task, it must actively include the sum of all human knowledge, and with it a plethora of representatives for the representation of reality.

The interrogations presented above examine how to focus on a robust, inclusive, and inviting community that can sustain what is, in many ways, an impossible project. There is a boldness to this ambition, of course. There is also a boldness to the idea that this process should and can happen within an inclusive and welcoming setting in order to invite the most diverse crowd of encyclopedia editors in history. What is at stake is exactly its project – what is included in the sum of all human knowledge? What counts as facts and truth, what counts as knowledge, and, in the end, whose reality gets represented? The answer lies in who gets to represent that reality, and whether that can shift, change, and grow. The reality that Wikipedia can represent depends on the realities and perspectives of the people allowed to contribute, and must be more inclusive to allow "the sum of all human knowledge." We believe Wikipedia can do this, and look forward to its future.

Notes

1 Steven L. Thorne, "Cultures-of-Use and Morphologies of Communicative Action," *Language Learning & Technology* 20, no. 2 (2016): 185, http://llt.msu.edu/issues/june 2016/thorne.pdf.
2 Roblimo, "Wikipedia Founder Jimmy Wales Responds," *Slashdot* (blog), July 28, 2004, https://slashdot.org/story/04/07/28/1351230/wikipedia-founder-jimmy-wales-responds.
3 For a fuller treatment of Wikipedia and misinformation, See: Zachary J. McDowell and Matthew A. Vetter, "It Takes a Village to Combat a Fake News Army: Wikipedia's Community and Policies for Information Literacy," *Social Media + Society* 6, no. 3 (July 1, 2020), https://doi.org/10.1177/2056305120937309.
4 Alex Pasternack, "How Wikipedia's Volunteers Became the Web's Best Weapon against Misinformation," *Fast Company*, March 7, 2020, https://www.fastcompany.com/90471667/how-wikipedia-volunteers-became-the-webs-best-weapon-against-misinformation.
5 Pete Forsyth, "How Wikipedia Dodged the Public Outcry Plaguing Social Media Platforms," *Medium*, December 2, 2019, https://misinfocon.com/wikipedia-built-to-battle-fake-news-c36370fe2c0e.
6 Sara Morrison, "How Wikipedia Is Preparing for Election Day," *Vox*, November 2, 2020, https://www.vox.com/recode/2020/11/2/21541880/wikipedia-presidential-election-misinformation-social-media.
7 Yochai Benkler, "From Utopia to Practice and Back," in *Wikipedia @ 20: Stories of an Incomplete Revolution*, eds. Joseph Reagle and Jackie Koerner (Cambridge: MIT Press, 2020), 47.
8 Shoshana Zuboff, *The Age of Surveillance Capitalism: The Fight for a Human Future at the New Frontier of Power*, First Trade Paperback Ed. (New York: PublicAffairs, 2020). "The Definition," n.p.
9 Ibid., 10.
10 Zuboff, "Surveillance Capitalism," 53.
11 R. Cooke, "Wikipedia Is the Last Best Place on the Internet," *Wired*, 2020, https://www.wired.com/story/wikipedia-online-encyclopedia-best-place-internet/.
12 Shoshana Zuboff, "You Are Now Remotely Controlled," *The New York Times*, January 24, 2020, Opinion, https://www.nytimes.com/2020/01/24/opinion/sunday/surveillance-capitalism.html.
13 Ibid.

14 Wikimedia Foundation, "Promoting Knowledge Equity," July 14, 2020, https://wikimediafoundation.org/our-work/education/promoting-knowledge-equity/.
15 Wikimedia Foundation, "Promoting Knowledge Equity."
16 Benkler, "From Utopia to Practice and Back," 47.
17 See Chapter 1 for our discussion on Wikipedia's Third Pillar: "Wikipedia is free content".
18 Brief description of 2030 vision.
19 "Strategy/Wikimedia Movement/2018-20 - Meta," *Wikimedia Foundation*, last modified January 14, 2021, https://meta.wikimedia.org/wiki/Strategy/Wikimedia_movement/2018-20.
20 "Strategy/Wikimedia Movement/2018-20 - Meta".
21 Bryce Peake, "WP:THREATENING2MEN:Misogynist Infopolitics and the Hegemony of the Asshole Consensus on English Wikipedia," *ADA, A Journal of Gender, New Media, and Technology*, no. 7 (April 2015), https://adanewmedia.org/2015/04/issue7-peake/
22 "Universal Code of Conduct - Meta," *Wikimedia Foundation*, last modified January 20, 2021, https://meta.wikimedia.org/wiki/Universal_Code_of_Conduct.
23 "Universal Code of Conduct - Meta," last modified January 20, 2021, https://meta.wikimedia.org/wiki/Universal_Code_of_Conduct.
24 Ibid.
25 "Universal Code of Conduct/Draft Review - Meta," last modified January 20, 2021, https://meta.wikimedia.org/wiki/Universal_Code_of_Conduct/Draft_review.
26 Ibid.
27 "Wikipedia: Assume Good Faith," *Wikipedia*, December 6, 2020, https://en.wikipedia.org/w/index.php?title=Wikipedia:Assume_good_faith&oldid=992724728.
28 "Wikipedia: Five Pillars," *Wikipedia*, December 27, 2020, https://en.wikipedia.org/w/index.php?title=Wikipedia:Five_pillars&oldid=996637443.
29 Zachary J. McDowell and Matthew A. Vetter, "It Takes a Village to Combat a Fake News Army: Wikipedia's Community and Policies for Information Literacy," *Social Media + Society* 6, no. 3 (July 1, 2020): https://doi.org/10.1177/2056305120937309
30 "Wikipedia: Assume Good Faith," *Wikipedia*, last modified December 6, 2020, https://en.wikipedia.org/w/index.php?title=Wikipedia:Assume_good_faith&oldid=985510496.
31 "Wikipedia: Please Do Not Bite the Newcomers," *Wikipedia*, January 22, 2021, https://en.wikipedia.org/w/index.php?title=Wikipedia:Please_do_not_bite_the_newcomers&oldid=1002019014.
32 See Chapters 3 and 4 for a more detailed discussion of Wikipedia's epistemological narrowness.
33 "Wikipedia: Five Pillars," *Wikipedia*, last modified December 7, 2020, https://en.wikipedia.org/w/index.php?title=Wikipedia:Five_pillars&oldid=977945932.
34 McDowell and Vetter, "It Takes a Village."

Bibliography

Alexa.com. "Wikipedia.Org Competitive Analysis, Marketing Mix and Traffic." Accessed January 5, 2021. https://www.alexa.com/siteinfo/wikipedia.org.

Barnett, Scot, and Casey Andrew Boyle, editors. *Rhetoric, through Everyday Things*. Rhetoric, Culture, and Social Critique. Tuscaloosa: The University of Alabama Press, 2016.

Benjakob, Omer. "Why Wikipedia Is Immune to Coronavirus." *Haaretz.com*. Accessed December 4, 2020. https://www.haaretz.com/us-news/.premium.MAGAZINE-why-wikipedia-is-immune-to-coronavirus-1.8751147.

Benkler, Yochai. "Coase's Penguin, or, Linux and 'The Nature of the Firm.'" *The Yale Law Journal* 112, no. 3 (2002): 369–446. https://doi.org/10.2307/1562247.

Benkler, Yochai. "From Utopia to Practice and Back." In *Wikipedia @ 20: Stories of an Incomplete Revolution*, edited by Joseph Reagle and Jackie Koerner, 43–54. Cambridge, MA: MIT Press, 2020.

Berger, Peter L., and Thomas Luckmann. *The Social Construction of Reality: A Treatise in the Sociology of Knowledge*. New York: Anchor, 1967.

Brown, Adam R. "Wikipedia as a Data Source for Political Scientists: Accuracy and Completeness of Coverage." *PS: Political Science and Politics* 44, no. 2 (2011): 339–343. https://www.jstor.org/stable/41319920.

Chomsky, Noam, and Michel Foucault. *The Chomsky-Foucault Debate: On Human Nature*. New York: The New Press, 2006.

"Citation Hunt." Accessed December 6, 2020. https://citationhunt.toolforge.org/en?id=1f50f263.

Clement, Alison. Twitter Post. January 30, 2010, 2:00 p.m. https://twitter.com/alisonclement/status/8421314259.

Cohen, Noam. "Define Gender Gap? Look Up Wikipedia's Contributor List." *The New York Times*. January 30, 2011. https://www.nytimes.com/2011/01/31/business/media/31link.html.

Cohen, Noam. "How Wikipedia Prevents the Spread of Coronavirus Misinformation." *Wired*. Accessed August 2, 2020. https://www.wired.com/story/how-wikipedia-prevents-spread-coronavirus-misinformation/.

Cohen, Noam. "The Latest on Virginia Tech, From Wikipedia." *The New York Times*. April 23, 2007. https://www.nytimes.com/2007/04/23/technology/23link.html.

Collier, Benjamin, and Julia Bear. "Conflict, Criticism, or Confidence: An Empirical Examination of the Gender Gap in Wikipedia Contributions." In *Proceedings of the ACM 2012 Conference on Computer Supported Cooperative Work*. New York, NY, USA. (2012): 383–392. https://doi.org/10.1145/2145204.2145265.

Cooke, R. "Wikipedia Is the Last Best Place on the Internet." *Wired*. 2020. https://www.wired.com/story/wikipedia-online-encyclopedia-best-place-internet/.

Creative Commons. "The Story of Creative Commons." Accessed December 30, 2020. https://certificates.creativecommons.org/cccertedu/chapter/1-1-the-story-of-creative-commons/.

Cunningham, Ward. "WikiWikiWeb." Accessed January 6, 2021. https://wiki.c2.com/.

Deleuze, Gilles, and Claire Parnet. *Dialogues*. New York: Columbia University Press, 1987, 69.

Diderot, Denis. "Encyclopedia." *The Encyclopedia of Diderot & d'Alembert Collaborative Translation Project*, Translated by Philip Stewart. Ann Arbor: Michigan Publishing, University of Michigan Library, 2002. http://hdl.handle.net/2027/spo.did2222.0000.004 (accessed January 5, 2020). Originally published as "Encyclopédie," *Encyclopédie ou Dictionnaire raisonné des sciences, des arts et des métiers*, 5:635–648A (Paris, 1755).

Ford, Heather, and Judy Wajcman. "'Anyone Can Edit', Not Everyone Does: Wikipedia's Infrastructure and the Gender Gap." *Social Studies of Science* 47, no. 4. (August 1, 2017): 511–27. https://doi.org/10.1177/0306312717692172.

Forsyth, Peter. "How Wikipedia Dodged the Public Outcry Plaguing Social Media Platforms." *Medium*. Accessed December 2, 2019. https://misinfocon.com/wikipedia-built-to-battle-fake-news-c36370fe2c0e.

Forsyth, Peter. "How Wikipedia Dodged Public Outcry Plaguing Social Media Platforms." *Wikistrategies.net*. Accessed August 23, 2018. https://wikistrategies.net/how-wikipedia-dodged-public-outcry-plaguing-social-media-platforms/.

Foucault, Michel. *The Archaeology of Knowledge & The Discourse on Language*. New York: Vintage, 1982.

Fox, Justin. "Academic Publishing Can't Remain Such a Great Business: Free Access to Research Is Coming Someday." November 3, 2015. https://www.bloomberg.com/opinion/articles/2015-11-03/academic-publishing-can-t-remain-such-a-great-business.

Gallert, Peter, and Maja Van der Velden. "Reliable Sources for Indigenous Knowledge: Dissecting Wikipedia's Catch-22." In *Embracing Indigenous Knowledge in a New Technology Design Paradigm*, edited by Nicola J. Bidwell and Heike Winschiers-Theophilus. Indigenous Knowledge Technology Conference, 2013. http://ir.nust.na/jspui/handle/10628/409.

Galloway, Alexander R. *The Interface Effect*. Cambridge, UK ; Malden, MA: Polity, 2012.

Geiger, R. Stuart. "The Lives of Bots." In *Critical Point of View: A Wikipedia Reader*, edited by Geert Lovink and Nathaniel Tkacz, 78–93. Amsterdam: Institute of Network Cultures, 2011.

Giles, Jim. "Internet Encyclopaedias Go Head to Head." *Nature* 438, no. 7070 (December 1, 2005): 900–901. https://doi.org/10.1038/438900a.

Gorman, Michael. "Jabberwiki: The Educational Response, Part II." *Encyclopedia Britannica Blog*. Accessed December 1, 2020. http://blogs.britannica.com/2007/06/jabberwiki-the-educational-response-part-ii/.

Graham, Mark. "Wiki Space: Palimpsests and the Politics of Exclusion." In *Critical Point of View: A Wikipedia Reader*, edited by Geert Lovink and Nathaniel Tkacz, 269–282. Amsterdam: Institute of Network Cultures, 2011. https://papers.ssrn.com/abstract=2075015.

Graells-Garrido, Eduardo, Mounia Lalmas, and Filippo Menczer, "First Women, Second Sex: Gender Bias in Wikipedia." In *Proceedings of the 26th ACM Conference on Hypertext & Social Media*. New York, NY, USA. (2015): 165–174. https://doi.org/10.1145/2700171.2791036.

Gramsci, Antonio. *Selections from the Prison Notebooks of Antonio Gramsci*. Edited and translated by Quintin Hoare and Geoffrey Nowell Smith. London: Lawrence and Wishart, 1971.

Gries, Laurie E. *Still Life with Rhetoric: A New Materialist Approach for Visual Rhetorics*. Logan: Utah State University Press, 2015.

Gruwell, Leigh. "Wikipedia's Politics of Exclusion: Gender, Epistemology, and Feminist Rhetorical (In)Action." *Computers and Composition* 37 (September 1, 2015): 117–131. https://doi.org/10.1016/j.compcom.2015.06.009.

Harrison, Stephen. "Happy 18th Birthday, Wikipedia. Let's Celebrate the Internet's Good Grown-Up." *Washington Post*. January 14, 2019. https://www.washingtonpost.com/opinions/happy-18th-birthday-wikipedia-lets-celebrate-the-internets-good-grown-up/2019/01/14/e4d854cc-1837-11e9-9ebf-c5fed1b7a081_story.html.

Hwang, Thomas J., Florence T. Bourgeois, and John D. Seeger. "Drug Safety in the Digital Age." *The New England Journal of Medicine* 370, no. 26 (June 26, 2014): 2460–2462. https://doi.org/10.1056/NEJMp1401767.

Ianucci, Rebecca. "What Can Fact-Checkers Learn from Wikipedia? We Asked the Boss of Its Nonprofit Owner." *Poynter* (blog). July 6, 2017. https://www.poynter.org/fact-checking/2017/what-can-fact-checkers-learn-from-wikipedia-we-asked-the-boss-of-its-nonprofit-owner/.

Jack, Carolyn. "Lexicon of Lies: Terms for Problematic Information." *Data & Society* 3 (2017): 1–20.

Jarvis, Claire. "A Deleted Wikipedia Page Speaks Volumes about Its Biggest Problem." *Fast Company*. April 25, 2019. https://www.fastcompany.com/90339700/a-deleted-wikipedia-page-speaks-volumes-about-its-biggest-problem.

Jiang, Jialei, and Matthew A. Vetter. "The Good, the Bot, and the Ugly: Problematic Information and Critical Media Literacy in the Postdigital Era." *Postdigital Science and Education* 2, no. 1 (2019): 78–94. https://doi.org/10.1007/s42438-019-00069-4.

Jowett, Garth, and Victoria O'Donnell. *Propaganda & Persuasion*. 7th ed. Los Angeles: SAGE, 2019.

Know Your Meme. "[Citation Needed]." Accessed January 21, 2021. https://knowyourmeme.com/memes/citation-needed.

Kräenbring, Jona, Tika Monzon Penza, Joanna Gutmann, Susanne Muehlich, Oliver Zolk, Leszek Wojnowski, Renke Maas, Stefan Engelhardt, and Antonio Sarikas. "Accuracy and Completeness of Drug Information in Wikipedia: A Comparison with Standard Textbooks of Pharmacology." *PLOS ONE* 9, no. 9 (September 24, 2014) https://doi.org/10.1371/journal.pone.0106930.

Kramer, Katrina. "Female Scientists' Pages Keep Disappearing from Wikipedia – What's Going on?" *Chemistry World*. Last modified July 3, 2019. https://www.chemistryworld.com/news/female-scientists-pages-keep-disappearing-from-wikipedia-whats-going-on/3010664.article.

Kriplean, Travis, Ivan Beschastnikh, David W. McDonald, and Scott A. Golder. "Community, Consensus, Coercion, Control: Cs*w or How Policy Mediates Mass Participation." In *Proceedings of the 2007 International ACM Conference on Supporting Group Work*. Sanibel Island, Florida, USA (2007): 167–176. https://doi.org/10.1145/1316624.1316648.

Leuf, Bo, and Ward Cunningham. *The Wiki Way: Quick Collaboration on the Web*. Boston: Addison-Wesley, 2001.

Lih, Andrew. *The Wikipedia Revolution: How a Bunch of Nobodies Created the World's Greatest Encyclopedia*. 1st ed. New York: Hyperion, 2009.

Maher, Katherine. Twitter Post. "Journalists — If You're Going to Come after @Wikipedia for Its Coverage of Women…" Twitter. October 3, 2018. https://twitter.com/krmaher/status/1047453672790093824.

Marx, Karl. *Das Kapital*. Edited by Friedrich Engels. Washington, DC: Regnery Publishing, 1996.

McDowell, Zachary J., and Matthew A. Vetter. "It Takes a Village to Combat a Fake News Army: Wikipedia's Community and Policies for Information Literacy." *Social Media + Society* 6, no. 3 (July 1, 2020): 1–13. https://doi.org/10.1177/2056305120937309.

Menking, Amanda, and Ingrid Erickson. "The Heart Work of Wikipedia: Gendered, Emotional Labor in the World's Largest Online Encyclopedia." In *Proceedings of the 33rd Annual ACM Conference on Human Factors in Computing Systems*." Seoul, Republic of Korea (2015): 207–210. https://doi.org/10.1145/2702123.2702514.

Menking, Amanda, Ingrid Erickson, and Wanda Pratt, "People Who Can Take It: How Women Wikipedians Negotiate and Navigate Safety." In *Proceedings of the 2019 CHI Conference on Human Factors in Computing Systems*. Glasgow, Scotland, UK (2019): 1–14. https://doi.org/10.1145/3290605.3300702.

Menking, Amanda, and Jon Rosenberg. "WP: NOT, WP: NPOV, and Other Stories Wikipedia Tells Us: A Feminist Critique of Wikipedia's Epistemology." *Science, Technology, & Human Values*. May 13, 2020. https://doi.org/10.1177/0162243920924783.

Morrison, Sara. "How Wikipedia Is Preparing for Election Day." *Vox*. November 2, 2020. https://www.vox.com/recode/2020/11/2/21541880/wikipedia-presidential-election-misinformation-social-media.

O'Sullivan, Dan. "What Is an Encyclopedia? A Brief Overview from Pliny to Wikipedia." In *Critical Point of View: A Wikipedia Reader*, edited by Geert Lovink and Nathaniel Tkacz, 34–49. Amsterdam: Institute of Network Cultures, 2011.

Panitch, Judith M., and Sarah Michalak. "The Serials Crisis: A White Paper for the UNC-Chapel Hill Scholarly Communications Convocation." Accessed December 18, 2020. https://ils.unc.edu/courses/2019_fall/inls700_001/Readings/Panitch2005-SerialsCrisis.htm.

Parikka, Jussi. *What Is Media Archaeology?* Cambridge, UK ; Malden, MA: Polity, 2012.

Pasternack, Alex. "How Wikipedia's Volunteers Became the Web's Best Weapon against Misinformation." *Fast Company*. March 7, 2020. https://www.fastcompany.com/90471667/how-wikipedia-volunteers-became-the-webs-best-weapon-against-misinformation.

Peake, Bryce. "WP: THREATENING2MEN: Misogynist Infopolitics and the Hegemony of the Asshole Consensus on English Wikipedia." *ADA, A Journal of Gender, New Media, and Technology*, no. 7 (April 2015). https://adanewmedia.org/2015/04/issue7-peake/

Qaiser, Farah. "Like Zika, The Public Is Heading To Wikipedia During The COVID-19 Coronavirus Pandemic." *Forbes*. Accessed August 2, 2020. https://www.forbes.com/sites/farahqaiser/2020/03/18/like-zika-the-public-is-heading-to-wikipedia-during-the-covid-19-coronavirus-pandemic/

Roblimo. "Wikipedia Founder Jimmy Wales Responds." *Slashdot* (blog), July 28, 2004. https://slashdot.org/story/04/07/28/1351230/wikipedia-founder-jimmy-wales-responds.

Sample, Ian. "Harvard University Says It Can't Afford Journal Publishers' Prices." *The Guardian*. April 24, 2012. http://www.theguardian.com/science/2012/apr/24/harvard-university-journal-publishers-prices.

Taraborelli, Dario. "Seven Years after Nature, Pilot Study Compares Wikipedia Favorably to Other Encyclopedias in Three Languages." *Diff* (blog). August 2, 2012. https://diff.wikimedia.org/2012/08/02/seven-years-after-nature-pilot-study-compares-wikipedia-favorably-to-other-encyclopedias-in-three-languages/.

Thalen, Mikael. "Meet the Wikipedia Editors Fighting to Keep Coronavirus Pages Accurate." *The Daily Dot*. March 24, 2020. https://www.dailydot.com/debug/wikipedia-coronavirus-page/.

Thorne, Steven L. "Cultures-of-Use and Morphologies of Communicative Action." *Language Learning & Technology* 20 no. 2 (2016): 185–191. http://llt.msu.edu/issues/june 2016/thorne.pdf.

Vetter, Matthew A. "Possible Enlightenments: Wikipedia's Encyclopedic Promise and Epistemological Failure." In *Wikipedia @ Twenty: Stories from an Incomplete Revolution*, edited by Joseph Reagle and Jackie Koerner, 285–295. Cambridge, MA: MIT Press, 2020.

Vetter, Matthew A., John Andelfinger, Shahla Asadolahi, Wenqi Cui, Jialei Jiang, Tyrone Jones, and Zeeshan F. Siddique. "Wikipedia's Gender Gap and Disciplinary Praxis: Representing Women Scholars in Digital Rhetoric and Writing Fields." *Journal of Multimodal Rhetorics* 2, no. 2 (2018): 6–22.

Vetter, Matthew A., Zachary J. McDowell, and Mahala Stewart. "From Opportunities to Outcomes: The Wikipedia-Based Writing Assignment." *Computers and Composition* 52 (June 1, 2019): 53–64. https://doi.org/10.1016/j.compcom.2019.01.008.

Wadewitz, Adrianne. "Wikipedia's Gender Gap and the Complicated Reality of Systemic Gender Bias." *HASTAC* (blog), 2013. https://www.hastac.org/blogs/wadewitz/2013/07/26/wikipedias-gender-gap-and-complicated-reality-systemic-gender-bias.

Wagner, Claudia, David Garcia, and Markus Strohmaier. "It's a Man's Wikipedia? Assessing Gender Inequality in an Online Encyclopedia." Palo Alto, CA: AAAI, 2015. 454–463. https://www.aaai.org/ocs/index.php/ICWSM/ICWSM15/paper/view/10585

Wagner, R. Polk. "Information Wants to Be Free: Intellectual Property and the Mythologies of Control." *Columbia Law Review* 103, no. 4 (2003): 995–1034.

Walker, Paul. "A Rhythmic Refrain: Britain's Mass-Observation as Rhetorical Assemblage." *Rhetoric Review* 35, no. 3 (July 2, 2016): 212–225. https://doi.org/10.1080/07350198.2016.1178690

Walling, Steven. "Why Wikipedians Are the Weirdest People on the Internet." *Ignite Portland*. 2010. https://www.youtube.com/watch?v=UEkF5o6KPNI.

WikiCred. "WikiCred." Accessed December 6, 2020. https://www.wikicred.org/

Wiki Education. "How Do Students Change Wikipedia?" Last modified May 31, 2016. https://wikiedu.org/changing/wikipedia/.

Wikimedia Foundation. "Harassment Survey." https://upload.wikimedia.org/wikipedia/commons/5/52/Harassment_Survey_2015_-_Results_Report.pdf.

Wikimedia Foundation. "Promoting Knowledge Equity." Accessed July 14, 2020. https://wikimediafoundation.org/our-work/education/promoting-knowledge-equity/

Wikimedia Foundation. "Strategy/Wikimedia Movement/2018–20- Meta." Last modified January 14, 2021. https://meta.wikimedia.org/wiki/Strategy/Wikimedia_movement/2018-20

Wikimedia Foundation. "Universal Code of Conduct/Draft Review - Meta." Last modified January 20, 2021. https://meta.wikimedia.org/wiki/Universal_Code_of_Conduct/Draft_review.

Wikimedia Foundation. "Universal Code of Conduct - Meta." Last modified January 20, 2021. https://meta.wikimedia.org/wiki/Universal_Code_of_Conduct.

Wikimedia Foundation. "Wikipedia and COVID-19." Accessed April 13, 2020. https://wikimediafoundation.org/covid19/data/.

Wikimedia Foundation. "Wikistats - Statistics for Wikimedia Projects." Last modified January 5, 2021. https://stats.wikimedia.org/#/en.wikipedia.org.

Wikimedia Foundation labs. "Gender by Wikipedia Language." *Wikipedia Human Gender Indicators*. Accessed June 9, 2015. https://whgi.wmflabs.org/gender-by-language.html.

Wikipedia, s.v. "1Lib1Ref." Last modified November 2, 2020. https://en.wikipedia.org/w/index.php?title=1Lib1Ref&oldid=986673021.

Wikipedia, s.v. "Category: All Articles with Unsourced Statements." Last modified October 12, 2020. https://en.wikipedia.org/w/index.php?title=Category:All_articles_with_unsourced_statements&oldid=983216779.

Wikipedia, s.v. "Encyclopædia Britannica." Last modified December 20, 2020. https://en.wikipedia.org/w/index.php?title=Encyclop%C3%A6dia_Britannica&oldid=995346575.

Wikipedia, s.v. "Free and Open-Source Software." Last modified December 25, 2020. https://en.wikipedia.org/w/index.php?title=Free_and_open-source_software&oldid=996259231.

Wikipedia, s.v. "History of Free and Open-Source Software." Last modified December 1, 2020. https://en.wikipedia.org/w/index.php?title=History_of_free_and_open-source_software&oldid=991662037.

Wikipedia, s.v. "Reliability of Wikipedia." Last modified July 17, 2020. https://en.wikipedia.org/w/index.php?title=Reliability_of_Wikipedia&oldid=968078346.

Wikipedia, s.v. "Systemic Bias." Last modified July 11, 2020. https://en.wikipedia.org/w/index.php?title=Systemic_bias&oldid=967204152.

Wikipedia, s.v. "The New York Times." Last modified December 2, 2020. https://en.wikipedia.org/w/index.php?title=The_New_York_Times&oldid=991895613.

Wikipedia, s.v. "Wikipedia: Articles for Deletion." Last modified November 21, 2020. https://en.wikipedia.org/w/index.php?title=Wikipedia:Articles_for_deletion&oldid=989883288

Wikipedia, s.v. "Wikipedia: Assume Good Faith." Last modified December 6, 2020. https://en.wikipedia.org/w/index.php?title=Wikipedia:Assume_good_faith&oldid=992724728.

Wikipedia, s.v. "Wikipedia: Be Bold." Last modified October 30, 2001. https://en.wikipedia.org/w/index.php?title=Wikipedia:Be_bold&oldid=238127.

Wikipedia, s.v. "Wikipedia: Be Bold." Last modified October 21, 2020. https://en.wikipedia.org/w/index.php?title=Wikipedia:Be_bold&oldid=984736314.

Wikipedia, s.v. "Wikipedia: Biographies of Living Persons." Last modified October 5, 2020. https://en.wikipedia.org/w/index.php?title=Wikipedia:Biographies_of_living_persons&oldid=981904218.

Wikipedia, s.v. "Wikipedia: Bot Policy." Last modified September 29, 2020. https://en.wikipedia.org/w/index.php?title=Wikipedia:Bot_policy&oldid=981013140.

Wikipedia, s.v. "Wikipedia: Bots." Last modified December 7, 2020. https://en.wikipedia.org/w/index.php?title=Wikipedia:Bots&oldid=992898959.

Wikipedia, s.v. "Wikipedia: Citation Needed." Last modified July 7, 2020. https://en.wikipedia.org/w/index.php?title=Wikipedia:Citation_needed&oldid=966577082.
Wikipedia, s.v. "Wikipedia: Consensus." Last modified October 14, 2020. https://en.wikipedia.org/w/index.php?title=Wikipedia:Consensus&oldid=983556771.
Wikipedia, s.v. "Wikipedia: Deletion Review/Log/2020 January 31." Last modified February 8, 2020. https://en.wikipedia.org/w/index.php?title=Wikipedia:Deletion_review/Log/2020_January_31&oldid=939731312.
Wikipedia, s.v. Wikipedia: FAQ/Copyright." Last modified August 29, 2020. https://en.wikipedia.org/w/index.php?title=Wikipedia:FAQ/Copyright&oldid=975545050.
Wikipedia, s.v. "Wikipedia: Five Pillars." Last modified December 27, 2020. https://en.wikipedia.org/w/index.php?title=Wikipedia:Five_pillars&oldid=996637443
Wikipedia, s.v. "Wikipedia: List of Bots by Number of Edits." Last modified March 3, 2020. https://en.wikipedia.org/w/index.php?title=Wikipedia:List_of_bots_by_number_of_edits&oldid=943632202
Wikipedia, s.v. "Wikipedia: Namespace." Last modified December 22, 2020. https://en.wikipedia.org/w/index.php?title=Wikipedia:Namespace&oldid=995798895.
Wikipedia, s.v. "Wikipedia: Neutral Point of View." Last modified July 12, 2020. https://en.wikipedia.org/w/index.php?title=Wikipedia:Neutral_point_of_view&oldid=967336587
Wikipedia, s.v. "Wikipedia: Neutral Point of View." Last modified November 10, 2001. https://en.wikipedia.org/w/index.php?title=Wikipedia:Neutral_point_of_view&oldid=334854039
Wikipedia, s.v. "Wikipedia: Neutral Point of View/FAQ." Last modified December 29, 2020. https://en.wikipedia.org/w/index.php?title=Wikipedia:Neutral_point_of_view/FAQ&oldid=996952192.
Wikipedia, s.v. "Wikipedia: Neutral Point of View/Noticeboard#Reparative Therapy." Last modified July 12, 2020. https://en.wikipedia.org/w/index.php?title=Wikipedia:Neutral_point_of_view/Noticeboard&oldid=967345749.
Wikipedia, s.v. "Wikipedia: Neutral Point of View/Noticeboard." Last modified July 12, 2020. https://en.wikipedia.org/w/index.php?title=Wikipedia:Neutral_point_of_view/Noticeboard&oldid=9673 45749
Wikipedia, s.v. "Wikipedia: Notability (People)." Last modified August 23, 2020. https://en.wikipedia.org/w/index.php?title=Wikipedia:Notability_(people)&oldid=974588424
Wikipedia, s.v. "Wikipedia: Notability." Last modified December 20, 2020. https://en.wikipedia.org/w/index.php?title=Wikipedia:Notability&oldid=995288718.

Wikipedia, s.v. "Wikipedia: Please Do Not Bite the Newcomers." Last modified January 22, 2021. https://en.wikipedia.org/w/index.php?title=Wikipedia:Please_do_not_bite_the_newcomers&oldid=995712413.

Wikipedia, s.v. "Wikipedia: Purpose." December 15, 2020. https://en.wikipedia.org/w/index.php?title=Wikipedia:Purpose&oldid=994329979.

Wikipedia, s.v. "Wikipedia: Reliable Sources." July 1, 2020. https://en.wikipedia.org/w/index.php?title=Wikipedia:Reliable_sources&oldid=965472450.

Wikipedia, s.v. "Wikipedia: Scope." Last modified May 20, 2019. https://en.wikipedia.org/w/index.php?title=Wikipedia:Scope&oldid=897922426.

Wikipedia, s.v. "Wikipedia: Size of Wikipedia." Last modified December 25, 2020. https://en.wikipedia.org/w/index.php?title=Wikipedia:Size_of_Wikipedia&oldid=996199067.

Wikipedia, s.v. "Wikipedia: Sockpuppetry." Last modified December 31, 2020. https://en.wikipedia.org/w/index.php?title=Wikipedia:Sock puppetry&oldid=997525229.

Wikipedia, s.v. "Wikipedia: Statistics." Last modified October 3, 2020. https://en.wikipedia.org/w/index.php?title=Wikipedia:Statistics&oldid=981585678.

Wikipedia, s.v. "Wikipedia: The Pope Is Catholic." Last modified September 6, 2020. https://en.wikipedia.org/w/index.php?title=Wikipedia:The_Pope_is_Catholic&oldid=977052665.

Wikipedia, s.v. "Wikipedia: User Access Levels." Last modified January 1, 2021. https://en.wikipedia.org/w/index.php?title=Wikipedia:User_access_levels&oldid=997595794.

Wikipedia, s.v. "Wikipedia: Verifiability." Last modified August 2, 2003. https://en.wikipedia.org/w/index.php?title=Wikipedia:Verifiability&oldid=1230640.

Wikipedia, s.v. "Wikipedia: Verifiability." Last modified November 29, 2020. https://en.wikipedia.org/w/index.php?title=Wikipedia:Verifiability&oldid=991232984.

Wikipedia, s.v. "Wikipedia: What to Include." Last modified August 16, 2019. https://en.wikipedia.org/w/index.php?title=Wikipedia:What_to_include&oldid=911131538.

Wikipedia, s.v. "Wikipedia: What Wikipedia Is Not." Last modified July 15, 2020. https://en.wikipedia.org/w/index.php?title=Wikipedia:What_Wikipedia_is_not&oldid=967817887.

Wikipedia, s.v. "Wikipedia: Why Most Sentences Should Be Cited." Last modified June 2, 2020. https://en.wikipedia.org/w/index.php?title=Wikipedia:Why_most_sentences_should_be_cited&oldid=960321257.

Wikipedia, s.v. "Wikipedia: Wikipedia Day." Last modified November 25, 2020. https://en.wikipedia.org/w/index.php?title=Wikipedia:Wikipedia_Day&oldid=990613284.

Wikipedia, s.v. "Wikipedia: Wikipedians." Last modified December 1, 2020. https://en.wikipedia.org/w/index.php?title=Wikipedia:Wikipedians&oldid=991744041.

Wikipedia, s.v. "Wikipedia: WikiProject Reliability." Last modified November 24, 2020. https://en.wikipedia.org/w/index.php?title=Wikipedia:WikiProject_Reliability&oldid=990325388.

Wikipedia, s.v. "Wikipedia: WikiProject Women in Red." Last modified November 20, 2020. https://en.wikipedia.org/w/index.php?title=Wikipedia:WikiProject_Women_in_Red&oldid=989654837.

Wikipedia, s.v. "Wikipedia: WikiProject Women in Red/Essays/Primer for AfD, AfC and PROD." Last modified September 22, 2020. https://en.wikipedia.org/w/index.php?title=Wikipedia:WikiProject_Women_in_Red/Essays/Primer_for_AfD, _AfC_and_PROD&oldid=979787246.

Wikipedia, s.v. "Wikipedia: You Do Need to Cite That the Sky Is Blue." Last modified June 2, 2020. https://en.wikipedia.org/w/index.php?title=Wikipedia:You_do_need_to_cite_that_the_sky_is_blue&oldid=960389350.

Wiktionary. "Fact." Accessed December 29, 2020. https://en.wiktionary.org/wiki/fact.

Williams, Raymond. *Marxism and Literature*. Oxford: Oxford University Press, 1977.

Xing, Jiawei, and Matthew Vetter. "Editing for Equity: Understanding Instructor Motivations for Integrating Cross-Disciplinary Wikipedia Assignments." *First Monday*. May 25, 2020. https://doi.org/10.5210/fm.v25i6.10575.

xkcd. "Wikipedian Protester." Accessed January 21, 2021. https://xkcd.com/285/.

Zuboff, Shoshana. *The Age of Surveillance Capitalism: The Fight for a Human Future at the New Frontier of Power*. First Trade Paperback Edition. New York: PublicAffairs, 2020.

Zuboff, Shoshana. "You Are Now Remotely Controlled." *New York Times*. Accessed January 24, 2020. https://www.nytimes.com/2020/01/24/opinion/sunday/surveillance-capitalism.html.

Index

Note: Page number followed by "n" refer to end notes.

Printed in the United States
by Baker & Taylor Publisher Services